Healing Activities Children in Grief

Activities suitable for support groups with grieving children, preteens, and teens

TABLE OF CONTENTS

There are two types of activities in this book: an opening activity and a main activity. The activities are numbered. The letter "A" following a number identifies the activity as an opening activity. An opening activity can be a book or an activity designed to promote discussion. The letter "B" following a number identifies the activity as a main activity that involves a specific topic or theme. When planning a group, first choose an activity from the Activity "A" section, and then choose an activity from the Activity "B" section. There are some "A" and "B" activities that work well together and they are grouped in a separate section titled "Combined A & B Activities."

Written and Published by Gay McWhorter, M.Ed., ADEC Certified Grief Counselor
Copyright © 2003
ISBN # 0-9763035-0-7

Cover & Inside Title Page Artwork by Artville • Clip Art by Hemera

A Message from the Author

My husband was electrocuted in our backyard in a tragic accident in 1988. My children were four and seven at the time of his death. We desperately wanted and needed a support system to guide us during this difficult time of grief and loss; however, we were not able to find a place to interact with other grieving families. I went back to school to get my Masters in Counseling and in my studies found such a place in Fort Worth, Texas: The WARM Place® *(What About Remembering Me)*. The agency was founded in 1989 by Peggy Bohme and Dr. John Richardson and their work continues to inspire me and others who work with grieving families. After completing my degree I was able to go to work at this wonderful place. I only wish that I could have found it in time for my children to attend. In my ten years at this agency I have seen so many people come to us in their deepest pain. When they leave they are in a better place: they are on the road to healing. Children are so often the forgotten mourners and I believe strongly that children can experience hope and healing when they have the opportunity to grieve in the supporting presence of others who share the same pain.

As a grief counselor, one of my responsibilities has been to develop activities for support groups. This book is a compilation of the favorite activities of many groups over the years. The activities in this book provide the tools to allow children to express their feelings, discuss their fears and concerns, and remember the loved one who died.

This book follows the group structure that is currently in place at The WARM Place. The children are grouped with other children who have experienced a similar death loss. There are parent loss, sibling loss and grandparent loss groups. The children are also grouped based on their age. The Children's groups are for 5 to 8-year-olds, Preteen groups are for 9 to 12-year-olds, and Teen groups are for 13 to 18-year-olds. The Children, Preteen and Teen groups are open-ended, with the participants staying in the program for as long as they choose to stay. A parent or guardian also attends a group support session while their child/children are in their group(s).

The activities in this book can be used in a multitude of group settings. They can be used in a grief agency, in a school or in a church group for kids in grief.

— Gay McWhorter

Children's Activities (Ages 5 - 8)

Children's Opening (A) Activities

Children's Activity #1A:
Make a **box of items**. This box should contain lots of items that children talk about when they remember their loved one: baseball, glasses, fishhook, telephone, cowboy hat, baseball cap, cross, hammer, apron, remote control, favorite sports team items, eyeglass case, airplane, playing cards, camera, baseball glove, aftershave, shin guards, tie, fish bobber, calculator, scrunchie, paintbrush, canteen, stethoscope, coffee mug, business card, keys, golf tee, newspaper, etc. Have the children pick out an item that reminds them of the person who died and tell why they think of their loved one when they see that object.

Children's Activity #2A:
Give each child 2 or 3 **pipe cleaners**. Have them bend the pipe cleaners into something that reminds them of the person who died. When they are finished, ask if anyone would like to share their art with the group.

Children's Activity #3A:
Give the children an assignment to bring in a **memento or item of the deceased's to share**. Give children a chance to talk about their item. Next, using the Polaroid camera, take a photo of each child holding their special possession (take the photo close up to the child) and then place this special photo in a photo holder/folder. The child can decorate this photo folder as they wish.

Children's Activity #4A:
Use small, **hand held blackboards** and have the children take turns by drawing a face on the board (with chalk) of how they feel tonight and have the other children guess that feeling.

Children's Activity #5A:
Face cards. Make four large feeling **face posters**. Use faces showing mad, sad, happy, and guilty feelings. Ask the children when they have felt the feeling on the poster. This works well with young children to encourage a discussion of feelings they have experienced since the death of their loved one.

Children's Activity #6A:
Play the song: "The Frog Song: Tell Me How You Feel" on the tape Friends of the Family by The Celebration Shop. This is a cute song for young children. It helps to start a discussion of what feelings they are experiencing.

Children's Activity #7A:
*Read: <u>Alice's Special Room</u> by Dick Gackenbach. This is a long book for young children so you may want to paraphrase some of the middle pages, while completely reading the first and last pages. This book talks about a little girl whose cat dies, and she tells Mom that the cat is in a special room. The mom keeps looking for the cat and then discovers the special room is in her heart.

Discussion: We want to talk about how it feels when we start forgetting things about the person who died. Everyone, even adults, starts to forget things. It makes us sad to forget things. There are some things we can do. One thing we can do is to make a memory box and fill it with special mementos and drawings and notes and photos. Other things might be to get your loved one's cologne/perfume and smell it from time to time. Another thing to do is to ask people (other parent might help with this) to tell you a story about the person who died. If there is a video with the person who died it might be helpful to watch it with family members. Another way to "not forget" is to talk about the person who died. Ask the children to share their very favorite memory. You might also ask what item of clothing reminds them of the person who died. What was the loved one's favorite thing to do? Did they have a favorite food? Did they have a favorite restaurant that the family went to a lot?

Children's Activity #8A:
*Read: <u>Daddy's Chair</u> by S. Lanton. This book tells about a boy who, after the funeral, while visitors are at his house, gets very upset that other people might sit in his Dad's chair. Later he finds that the chair is a special place to remember his dad. Discuss: Is there any place at home where the child can go and remember his/her parent like the children in this book?

Children's Activity #9A:
*Read: <u>Feelings Inside You and Outloud Too</u> by B. Polland. This is a simple book with a page for each feeling. It has a question on each page to stimulate discussion. If you have specific feelings that you want your group to discuss you might want to pick out in advance which feeling words you want to address. It is a good book to stimulate discussion for the children.

Children's Activity #10A:
*Read: <u>Geranium Morning</u> by S. Powell. Discuss. This book deals with two classmates, one whose father has died and another whose mother is dying of cancer. Timothy and his father did a lot of things together, including working in the nursery. Every spring Timothy's dad got new geraniums to add to his collection. Usually Timothy went with his dad to get the geraniums, but one morning Timothy wanted to stay in bed. He told his dad he would wait until he returned and then have cocoa with him—another geranium morning tradition. However, Timothy never got his cocoa because his father was killed in a car accident. Timothy begins to hate Saturday mornings and cocoa. His mother also had difficulty dealing with this unexpected tragedy. "If only..." was the phrase Timothy kept thinking over and over again. If only he had gone with his dad. If only his dad hadn't wanted geraniums. No one seems to understand Timothy's feelings except Frannie, whose mother is dying. The story tells how the two children help each other deal with the death of their parents. Some discussion questions: *What things are different for this boy now that Dad has died? *What secret did the boy have that was bothering him? *Why didn't the boy want to go to the zoo? *What happened when he talked to Frannie?

Children's Activity #11A:
*Read: <u>Grandad Bill's Song</u> by Jane Yolen. This story tells of a boy's struggle to express his feelings following the death of his beloved grandfather.

Children's Activity #12A:
Read: <u>Grandma's Scrapbook</u> by Josephine Nobisso. After her grandmother dies, the memory of her legacy of love brings comfort through the pictures and mementos of her scrapbook.

Children's Activity #13A:
*Read: <u>I Know I Made It Happen</u> by Lynn Blackburn. This is a helpful book that directly addresses the issue of guilt in children. "I made it happen" thoughts are often an attempt to find a cause when important things happen. This book explains that things do not happen because we think bad thoughts. Many times a child feels responsible for a death because at some time he wished bad things about that person.

Children's Activity #14A:
*Read: <u>I'll Always Love You</u> by Hans Wilhelm. This is a story about the relationship between a boy and his dog, Elfie. As the years go by, the boy grows up and Elfie grows older. One night, Elfie dies in her sleep. The boy is comforted by the thought that every night he told Elfie, "I'll always love you."

Children's Activity #15A:
*Read: <u>It Must Hurt a Lot</u> by D. Sanford. Joshua's dog Muffin is killed, and Joshua hurts more than he has ever hurt before. But, with time, Joshua finds he has gained important secrets he can grow on.

Children's Activity #16A:
*Read: <u>Lost and Found: Remembering a Sister</u> by Ellen Yeomans. A young girl searches for understanding after the death of her sister. When she is told they lost her sister, she wonders if someone who is lost can also be found. This book shows the confusing thoughts and feelings this girl experiences following the death of her sister and the number of ways she continues to feel her sister's love.

Children's Activity #17A:
*Read: <u>Molly's Mom Died</u> by Margaret Holmes. This book talks about the feelings that Molly has experienced since the death of her mother.

Children's Activity #18A:
*Read: <u>My Grandma Leonie</u> by Bijou Le Tord. In this book a small boy reminisces about the special things he and Grandma Leonie did together. Grandma gets sick and goes to the hospital but never returns, and the boy misses his Grandma Leonie.

Children's Activity #19A:
*Read: <u>My Grandson Lew</u> by Charlotte Zolotow. In this book Lewis misses his grandfather even though he died when he was just two. Since the boy was so young his mother never told him that his grandfather died; she just stopped talking about him. The boy and his mother find that they both have lots of memories and that remembering Grandpa together is less lonely than each remembering him alone.

Children's Activity #20A:
*Read: <u>My Many Colored Days</u> by Dr. Seuss. This book describes each day in terms of a particular color, which in turn is associated with a specific emotion. Discuss how days before the death might be a different color than days after the death or different days are different colors. What color is their day today?

Children's Activity #21A:
*Read: <u>Some of the Pieces</u> by M. Madenski. This book looks at a family a year after the father's death. They can now look back and see that they have times when they are sad, but it isn't the intense pain as it was when Dad first died. It also talks about the importance of memories. This book also deals with the issue of spreading cremains.

Children's Activity #22A:
*Read: <u>Sometimes I Feel Like a Storm Cloud</u> by Lezlie Evans. This is a really cute book where a child describes how it feels to experience a variety of emotions.

Children's Activity #23A:
*Read: <u>Someone Special Died</u> by J.S. Prestine. The book tells the story of a young girl who wonders what life will be like when someone she loves dies. It includes what happens to the body and ways to remember the person who died.

Children's Activity #24A:
*Read: <u>Stacy Had a Little Sister</u> by Wendie C. Old. Stacy has mixed feelings about her new sister, Ashley. When the baby dies of sudden death syndrome, Stacy is sad and misses her.

Children's Activity #25A:
*Read: <u>The Saddest Time</u> by Norma Simon. Three poems about death separate each of the stories about a death. The first story is about Uncle Joe who dies while he is still relatively young. The second story is about a young boy who dies as a result of an accident. The third story is about a grandmother who is ill and eventually dies. The book conveys the idea that death can happen at any age.

Children's Activity #26A:
*Read: <u>Toby</u> by Margaret Wild. This is a story about a dog named Toby who is old and sick. The children become aware that he is getting weaker and weaker. The siblings in the family react differently to the dog's illness and death. Discussion topic: Have family members in their house reacted differently to their loved one's death?

Children's Activity #27A:
*Read: <u>Tough Boris</u> by M. Fox. This book is about a tough pirate whose parrot dies, and we find that even a tough, mean pirate cries. There are not a lot of words in this book but it is very cute so the "reader" needs to read this with a lot of feeling and expression.

Children's Activity #28A:
*Read: <u>When Dinosaurs Die: A Guide to Understanding Death</u> by Laurie Krasny Brown and Marc Brown. This book explains in simple language the feelings children may have regarding the death of a loved one and the ways to honor the memory of someone who has died.

Children's Activity #29A:
*Read: <u>When Someone Dies</u> by Sharon Greenlee. This simple book offers help in dealing with the confusion and hurt felt by children and adults following the death of a loved one. The author encourages her readers to remember the good times to help transform sorrow into comfort.

Children's Activity #30A:
*Read: <u>Where's Jess?</u> by Joy Johnson. This is a simple book that answers the questions and concerns of children following the death of a brother or sister.

Children's Activity #31A:
*Read: <u>Why Do People Die?</u> by Cynthia MacGregor. This book answers the questions children commonly ask after a death.

Children's Main (B) Activities

Children's Activity #1B:
Make a **ribbon in memory** of the loved one who died, using wide ribbon and magic markers. At the end of the evening place the ribbons on a tree or in a special place where your group meets. Create a ceremony as each child ties the ribbon on the tree or special place.

Children's Activity #2B:
(This activity is helpful for memories and anger.) Have the children draw on **pillowcases**. On one side, the children can draw all the happy memories that they can remember of their loved one. On the other side, the children draw all the things that have made them angry about the death. Make sure the children use permanent markers. Put a paper bag inside the pillowcase so that the colors do not go on to the other side. Explain to the children that when they get home they should put their pillow in this pillowcase. When they are angry, hit the bed with the angry side of the pillowcase. Then at night, to have happy thoughts, sleep with the memory side up. On the hem of the "happy" side of the pillowcase the children can autograph each other's pillowcase, if they so choose.

Children's Activity #3B:
"Remember" the loved one by making **a memory heart.** Materials needed: 1 piece of construction paper in red or pink (8 x 12 size) for the background, one long strip (1 1/2" x 18") for each child for the heart; and 10 pre-cut red strips (1 1/2" x 8") for inside the heart, scotch tape, scissors, and glue. Have the child choose a background sheet of construction paper. Take the long strip of construction paper and tape the ends together, then make a fold at the midpoint of the strip to form a heart. Tape this heart to the background sheet of construction paper. Then take the smaller pre-cut pieces of paper and write a happy memory, a message to their loved one, or a special thing about the loved one who died. Then curl them, and put them into the center of the heart to fill it. When all ten pieces are in the heart, they will not fall out. Some children may need help writing, and facilitators will need to provide help as needed.

Children's Activity #4B:
Give each child a piece of sturdy paper. Have them trace their hand on the paper and then cut it out. On the palm of the hand, have them put their loved one's name or the relationship (Dad, Mom, Sister, Grandparent, etc). On each "finger" put things that they remember about the loved one. After they have finished their drawing, staple a Popsicle stick on the hand (at the wrist). Then as a group **"wave" your hands** saying goodbye to the loved one. Remind the children that saying goodbye is not the same as forgetting.

Children's Activity #5B:

Make and pass out a "**Me, Myself, and I**" poster to each child. This poster can have a variety of topics to color and/or cut out pictures from a magazine. (Topics can be: These are some of the things I used to do with my loved one; This is a picture of my family; These are my friends; My favorite memory with my loved one; and This is how I feel tonight.) Also include in this poster a section to include the child's height and weight and "facts" about the child such as favorite food, color and hobbies.

Children's Activity #6B:

Have the children make **sock puppets**. Supplies: tube sock (1 per child), yarn for hair, buttons or eyes for eyes, red felt for mouth, black, brown, and yellow felt for eyebrows, mustaches, etc. and sticky glue. You will need a hot glue gun for the yarn for the hair (this is to be used by the adults only). After the children have made the puppets encourage a discussion of (choose one topic):
- Reaction to being told of the death
- Last memory of person who died
- How they are feeling tonight
- Special memory with loved one

Children's Activity #7B:

Take a **large piece of butcher paper** and cover the walls with the paper (The number of children you have will determine how much paper is needed). Let each child have a 2-3 foot space in front of the paper and give them magic markers. All at the same time have the children draw a picture of what they remember about the day their loved one died. Some may have seen the person die, others may have had someone bring them the news of the death. After they have finished, let the children explain their drawing.

Children's Activity #8B:

Purchase "**design a mugs**" for the children. These are special mugs into which the child can slip a paper in a special sleeve of the mug and enjoy the picture as he uses his/her mug. The children will draw a picture of a favorite memory with their loved one and then put it in the cup. The children can also add a photo at home.

Children's Activity #9B:

Using the **sidewalk chalk** let the children draw on the sidewalk coming up to your center. Let them draw something special for the loved one who died or have them draw a special memory.

Children's Activity #10B:

Have the children draw a **now and then** or **before and after** picture. Supplies: manila paper, markers, crayons, magazines, scissors, glue stick. Take a large piece of manila paper and draw a line down the middle. On one side of the paper the children will draw/cut out of magazines pictures that remind them of their family before the death and on the other side, pictures or a drawing of after the death. This can be a drawing of what the family looks like **now and then** or a special event or memory that happened **before** the death **and after** the death. While they are working on the pictures, encourage a discussion of what has changed and what is the same.

Children's Activity #11B:

Balloon launch. Give each child a helium balloon and a tag with a string. Let each child write a message on the tag and then tie it to the balloon. As a group, go outside and "launch" the balloons together and watch them as they float into the sky. This can be used for special occasions or on special days like birthdays and anniversaries.

Children's Activity #12B:

Polaroid feeling poster activity. Encourage a discussion about the feelings we have felt since our loved one died. Ask the children to think of a feeling they have felt and "show" us what they look like when they feel that feeling. Using the Polaroid camera, take a photo of each child as he/she "shows" us the feelings they have felt since the death. Use a poster board (18 x 24) and mount these photos on the poster and write the feeling the child is showing under the photo.

Children's Activity #13B:

Use **phones** and let the children "tell someone how they are feeling tonight" and then the adults, using the phones, role play a response back to the child.

Children's Activity #14B:

Make **body pictures**. Discuss first: has anyone had parts of his/her body hurt since the death? Sometimes it feels like our heart hurts, sometimes our eyes hurt from crying or from trying not to cry. Sometimes stomachs hurt. Sometimes heads hurt. Sometimes even legs or arms hurt. Tell the children that sometimes grieving can make you feel sick. Using large pieces of butcher paper, have each child lie on the paper and trace the child's body. Have the children color their "body" including making the face the way they are feeling tonight. Pass out Band-Aids and let the children place 1 or 2 Band-Aids on their bodies where they hurt.

Children's Activity #15B:

Make "**balloon people.**" The idea is that they will make this balloon "person" to show how they feel tonight. Each child will get balloon feet (cardboard cut in the shape of feet) and a balloon. First have the child color/decorate their "feet" with markers. You can also punch holes and have yarn available for those who want to put shoelaces in their feet. Next, help the children blow up a balloon and tie it. Push the knotted end of the balloon into the feet so the balloon person will stand up. Next, have the child use washable marking pens to draw their facial features on the balloon, encouraging them to draw how they feel tonight.

Children's Activity #16B:

Make a **secret thoughts pouch**. Explain to the children that this is a special pouch to keep someplace special to help keep their private thoughts. After the children have made (and decorated) their pouches, they can write or draw their secret thoughts on a piece of paper and hide it in the pouch. They could write things that make them mad, things that people have said, write or draw something for the person who died, or write things that they are worried about. When they get home, encourage them to find a place where they could hide their secret thoughts pouch. Whenever they think of something, they can add it to the pouch. Supplies needed: paper, crayons, hole puncher, yarn, little pieces of paper (for secret thoughts/pictures) and magic markers.

Children's Activity #17B:

When a new child comes to your group, give him/her a **coloring book** or journal book. For this age group I recommend <u>How I Feel: A Coloring Book for Grieving Children.</u> This is especially helpful for young children to color along with their parents. If you pass out a journal book, encourage them to add photographs and mementos to this book. It can be helpful for the child to ask the adults in his life to also add to this journal book.

Children's Combined A and B Activities

Children's Activity (A&B) #1:

*Read: <u>The Memory Box</u> by Kirsten McLaughlin. In this book the boy's grandfather dies unexpectedly. At first the boy is angry that his grandfather broke a promise to take him fishing on Wednesday. Then he is sad about all of the things he is going to miss doing with Grandpa. The boy decides to make a memory box. He fills his box with all sorts of special items that remind him of times he spent with his grandfather. When he shares it with his mother he smiles as he remembers special times with his Grandpa.

Make **memory boxes**. These are to be used to place a special item that the loved one who died may have given the child, or mementos of special times, or this could be a place to put notes or drawings to the deceased. Pass out a white cardboard box to each child. Use markers and encourage the children to decorate all of the sides of the box by drawing memories about the person who died, messages to the person who died, or a picture of what the family looked like before the death, etc. We have also made memory boxes by using pencil boxes or cigar boxes and having the children cut things from magazines that remind them of their loved one. We have found that the younger children have an easier time with the first type of memory box, while the older children enjoy making the second type of memory box.

Children's Activity (A&B) #2:

*Read: <u>Liplap's Wish</u> by J. London. After Liplap's grandmother dies, his mother tells him the ancient bunny legend about stars coming out at night to remind us that our loved ones shine forever in our hearts. Discussion topics: What were some of the ways the rabbit was feeling? What special things about Grandmother did Liplap remember? What is the significance of the star? (You can think of the person who died when you look at a star and know that that person will always be with us in a special way.)

Place a large glow-in-the-dark **star** in the children's group room. Turn out the lights, close the shades, and let each child make a wish on the star or use the star to say what they would like to say if they had one more chance to talk to the person who died. The stars will remind us that our loved ones always remain in our hearts. Then give each child a star to take home and put on the ceiling of his/her bedroom and use it to talk to the person who has died. This star can be an opportunity to say what they wanted to say.

Children's Activity (A&B) #3:

*Read: <u>Animal Crackers</u> by Bridget Marshall. This is a book about a grandmother who hid animal crackers and M&M's for her grandchildren to discover when they came to visit. At the funeral animal crackers were passed around to those who came to say good-bye to Nanny. The animal crackers helped everyone to remember Nanny.

Pass out animal crackers to the children and have them share something special they remember about their loved one who died.

Children's Activity (A&B) #4:

*Play the video <u>The Tenth Good Thing about Barney</u> or read the book by the same name by Judith Viorst. In this video/book, the boy's cat, Barney, dies. The boy is very sad and Mom has a great idea to have a funeral for Barney. Then the family comes up with ten good things about Barney. This helps the boy remember special things about Barney. Discussion topics: *How did the boy feel at the start of the video? (sad) *How did you know he felt that way? (didn't eat dinner or chocolate pudding, didn't watch TV, didn't read his book)*What did the boy's mother suggest to help him feel better? (have a funeral, think of ten good things about Barney)*What were some of the good things the boy thought of Barney? (brave, smart, funny, cuddly, etc.)

Have the children **make a list** of the ten good things about their loved one. Some of the children may need help writing the ten things about the loved one. (For example: Mom made chocolate chip cookies, she tucked me into bed every night, she read me a story, Dad took me fishing, etc.)

Children's Activity (A&B) #5:

*Read: <u>Double-Dip Feelings</u> by Barbara S. Cain, M.S.W. This book talks about times when we sometimes feel two feelings at the same time. Talk about times they have had double-dip feelings. They may have these feelings about coming to a support group; anxious about coming, but happy when they make new friends; or about closing at their group, happy that they can remember their loved one without coming to group, but sad to leave new friends. Sometimes when we have "double dip" feelings, we show one feeling and hide the other.

*Activity: Paper plate feelings activity.** Pass out paper plates. On one side of the plate the child draws a picture of his/her face showing a feeling he "shows" and on the other side he draws a picture of one of the feelings he "hides". Another option is to have the child draw two feelings that he is currently feeling. Use yarn, glue, magic markers, scissors, paper plates, and tongue depressor sticks. Have the children put the plates in front of their face and have each other guess both sides of the plates. (Use the tongue depressor sticks as a holder on the plate).

Children's Activity (A&B) #6:

*Read: <u>Today I Feel Silly</u> by Jamie Lee Curtis. This is a cute book that looks at some of the feelings children experience.

A **doll** with changeable faces is available for purchase with this book. Encourage the children to pick one of the changeable faces and put on the doll as he/she explains when he/she has felt that feeling.

Children's Activity (A&B) #7:

*Read: <u>The Garden Angel</u> by Jan Czech. This is a story about how a young child remembers grandpa's love as she plants a garden.

Life involves things growing and everything will at some point die. This activity is to **plant a seed**. Ask the children what will happen to this seed. *What does this seed need to grow? *Will this seed live forever? Part of this activity is the lesson that everything will die, even a seed, but another part of this activity is that we will make this flower for someone special in our lives. We will decorate the flower pots and plant a seed and then watch it grow and give this to a special person. Leave this open to the children. It could be something that the children bring to the cemetery, it could be for a surviving parent, or it could be for a special friend who has helped them in their grief journey. They need to decorate the pot before they plant the seeds in the dirt. Supplies: paint, brushes, soil, pot, Styrofoam 6" plate and one packet of seeds. Divide the seeds from the packet so that each child gets the same amount of seeds. Watch to make sure the child puts the seeds about 1" from the top. Water slightly.

Children's Activity (A&B) #8:

*Read: <u>A Terrible Thing Happened</u> by Margaret Holmes. The "terrible" thing that the boy experienced is never identified, which leaves it for the group to talk about. Discussion topics: What do the children think the boy "saw" or experienced? What is the terrible thing in their life that they have seen or experienced? This book is also good to show children that their anger is related to the "terrible" thing.

*Main Activity: Have the children **draw a picture** (like in the book) of what was terrible for them.

Children's Activity (A&B) #9:

*Read: <u>When Something Terrible Happens</u> by Marge Heegaard. This book can be used for discussion or as a coloring/journal book. It was designed to help children understand and cope with the overwhelming feelings from loss and change.

Have the children color the **"paper doll"** (see pages 12-13 in the book). This is to help the children express with colored crayons what they are experiencing and also show us where in their body they are feeling these feelings.

Children's Activity (A&B) #10:

*Read: <u>It's Not Your Fault</u> by J. Flynn. This is a good book that helps us reassure the children about the fact that they didn't do anything to make the person die. Children often connect things that are not logically connected or perhaps they don't know that there was nothing anyone could do to keep their loved one alive. Children need to be reassured that they did not make their loved one die.

After you have discussed the book, there is a page where the children can fill in the blanks on a **letter** to the person who died. Work with the children and help them as necessary.

Children's Activity (A&B) #11:

*Read: <u>I Was So Mad</u> by Mercer Mayer. In this simple book Little Critter is mad about some things. Discuss what things make the children angry and what they have done to help themselves feel better. Children need ways to cope with feelings that work for them. Discussion topics: *What things make Little Critter mad? *What things did Little Critter do to help him feel better?
Next, we have several anger releasing activities for the children to choose from.

Make "Angry Faces" on paper plate masks. Play music, "I get so mad," on the "Mr. Al Sings: Friends and Feelings" tape by Melody House. Let children dance to the music and hold up their masks when the song says, "I get so mad." Talk about what is OK to do when you are mad and what is not OK to do. Supplies needed: Plain white paper plates, Popsicle sticks or tongue depressors, markers or crayons, and yarn or strips of paper in yellow, brown, and black: Decorate with the yarn or strips of paper for hair. The Popsicle stick is glued at the bottom when the face is complete and is used as a handle for the children to hold the mask in front of their face.

Ice cube throw. Get a paper cup for each child and fill with ice cubes. Take the children outside and get into small groups. Have the children take an ice cube and throw it at a wall or down on the ground. When they throw the ice cube they are to say something that they are angry about. Talk about "What makes you mad?" and "What can you do when you feel mad?" You may also be able to identify feelings underneath the anger, like sadness or loneliness.

Balloon stomp. This is a "fun" anger activity. Blow up a balloon for each child. Use a ribbon and tie a balloon to each child's ankle. Go outside and have the children pop each other's balloons by stomping on them.

Take the children outside and let them **smash soda cans**. When they stomp on the can encourage them to name what they are angry at. They can step on the cans and walk around "smooshing" the cans as they walk.

Have **bubble wrap** available for the children to "stomp" on to release anger.

Children's Activity (A&B) #12:

*Read: <u>The Hurt</u> by Teddi Doleski. In this book Justin has a hurt. By not talking about his hurt, it gets bigger and bigger until it surrounds him. When he talks to his father, he finds the hurt can get smaller. Discussion topics: How hurt and sad/mad feelings can feel bigger and bigger, can get in the way, and prevent sleeping. How do they affect you? What did Justin do that finally helped (talked to his Dad)? What do you do when hurt gets big?

Let the children **blow up balloons** to represent their hurt. Have them name their hurt. Have them blow up the balloon and hold onto the balloons (don't tie) and let them go together or one by one.

Children's Activity (A&B) #13:

*Read: <u>The Accident</u> by Carol Carrick. In this book, Christopher's dog dies. A car hits Bodger, the dog, accidentally. Christopher was angry that the man hit his dog, even though it was not his fault because the dog ran out in front of the truck. The next morning Christopher wakes up, and for a minute forgets the dog has died. Then he remembers and is very sad. Dad buried the dog and Christopher was very angry that Dad did not let him help. So Christopher and Dad search for a stone to mark the grave and have a mini-funeral, by talking about fun memories. There is a lot in this book that may be similar to the feelings, events, etc. when a loved one dies. Discuss.

Give each child a smooth, 3" river rock or shell and using acrylic paints, have them **paint a** rock or shell for his loved one. Place the rock/shells in a special place at your agency (around a special tree, in a memorial garden, etc.) After the rock is painted, a facilitator should spray the rocks with the fixative spray. If dry before the children leave, lay the rocks around the special place as the child says their loved one's name.

Children's Activity (A&B) #14:

*Read: <u>Saying Goodbye to Daddy</u> by J.Vigna. In this book the girl's father died unexpectedly, and Mom and Grandfather help her understand what happens at a funeral and they remember special times with Dad. Discuss the book. Some possible questions could be: *Why was the lake house special to Clare? *Was Clare angry in the book? *Why was she angry? *Did Clare blame herself for her daddy's death? *Did dropping daddy's coffee cup or getting mad at him cause her father's accident? *What worried Clare? (What if mommy dies, too?) *Why did Clare put the chocolate chip cookie in the casket? *How did Clare feel when she and mommy found things in daddy's wallet? *Does anyone remember any of the same feelings Clare had?

The book leads in quite well to a discussion of what the children did for their loved one's funeral. Using **felt pieces** and a flannel board let the children show what happened at the funeral or memorial service. You may want to talk about funerals in general and ask each child to share what they remember about their loved one's funeral. Did the children do anything special at the funeral? Did anyone place something in the casket? **Note**: prior to group make felt pieces of all of the items a child might see at a funeral: casket, floral sprays for the casket, tall floral arrangements that are arranged at the side of the casket, hearse, people, an urn, etc.

Have the children **draw** a picture of what they remember about the funeral.

Children's Activity (A&B) #15:

*Read: <u>Love is a Family</u> by Roma Downey. This book tells of a little girl preparing for Family Fun night at her school. She is worried what the other children will say because she feels that her family is different from all the other children's families because she just has a mother. She finds that a family should not be defined by mother, father, and child, but by love.

Prior to group make **felt people and animals**. Have each child show on a felt board what their family looks like. (For a family with a mom and two children, the child would place a woman and two children and maybe a pet on the felt board). Make pets that the children can also include in this demonstration (cats, dogs, birds, fish, turtle, bunny, and hamster). The important message for the children is that everyone's family is different, but it is still a family. It would be helpful to normalize that there are places where they are aware that their family is different.

Children's Activity (A&B) #16:

*Read: <u>How to Get Rid of Bad Dreams</u> by Nancy Hazbry and Roy Condry. The idea of this book is for the children to find a plan or rehearsal of a different ending to their nightmare. Have the children draw a picture of their dream or nightmare as they remember it. When they are working on the picture discuss with the children a different ending for the dream. How would they like it to end? Some suggestions: someone coming to the rescue (superheroes), thinking of a way they are strong, or Mom/Dad protecting them.

Make **dream catchers**. The Chippewa Indians have a tradition that if you hang a dream catcher over you while you sleep, the dream catcher will catch the bad dreams in the web and daylight will make the bad dreams go away. For this activity each child will need a paper plate (first cut out the center of the plate and punch holes around the edge of the plate), magic markers, yarn, glue, feathers, beads (allow 20 beads per child), and a big eye needle. The children can decorate the plate. Using the yarn threaded in a large needle, have the children go back and forth across the paper plate (creating a web-type appearance) until all the holes are used. Then have the children put the beads on the catcher. The last bead will need to be tied to the string because a knot doesn't hold the beads. The feathers are then stuck in the beads using a small drop of glue. While working on this dream catcher, encourage a discussion of dreams, good and bad. Before the group leaves, have a show and tell of the dream catchers and tell the legend of the dream catcher to the group.

Children's Activity (A&B) #17:

*Read: <u>Lifetimes</u> by B. Mellonie and R. Ingpen. All lifetimes, whether long or short, have beginnings and endings and living in between. This book examines in simple terms how to deal with the feelings of grief when people or pets die.

Put together a **tray of things**. Put some things that are alive (a fish, a bug, a plant), some that are dead (have a dead fish, dead bug, and dried up dead leaf), some that are pretend things (stuffed animal). Discuss: How do they know if something is alive? How do they know the fish/bug is dead? What about the stuffed animals-have they ever been alive? Have a **stethoscope** to let the children hear for themselves that they are alive.

Children's Activity (A&B) #18:

*Read: <u>The Dead Bird</u> by M.W. Brown & R. Charlip. This is a simple book about a group of children who are in a park and find a dead bird. Discussion: *How did the children know the bird was dead? *How did the children feel? *What did they do? *Is this anything like what they do when a person dies? *How did the children show they cared for the bird? *Can you think of anything else they could have done or that you would have done?

Using **felt pieces** representing the characters in the book have the children **retell** the story. Another option is to let the children tell the story and change it in some way.

Children's Activity (A&B) #19:

*Discuss: Many children find it is hard to talk about the death. We want them to know that we understand it is hard to talk about the death and the person who died, and we admire their courage for all the hard work that they do. Discussion topics: *Why it might be hard to come to a support group? *How do they feel about coming? *How has coming to a support group helped?

Next, have the children make a **"badge of honor"** for the hard work they do. Give each child a badge that you have created for the children to color. You will need to have a hole punch and ribbon so that the children can hang these around their necks. Use magic markers to color the badges and zig-zag scissors to make a fancy cut around the badge.

Children's Activity (A&B) #20:

*Read: <u>I Heard Your Mommy Died,</u> or <u>I Heard Your Daddy Died</u> by M. Scrivani. These books talk about the different feelings children experience following the death of a mother/father. While the stories are similar, they do hit on things specific to each loss.

In the book, it talks about **drawing a picture** of the parent who died to put in their room. Let the child draw a picture of the parent. It can be a picture (to the best of their ability) of what the parent looked like, or a special memory or event.

Children's Activity (A&B) #21:

*Read: <u>The Snowman</u> by Robin Helen Vogel. This is a cute story about two brothers talking about Dad's death as they build a snowman. This is a good story for winter. You might condense the wording a little as you read this story to younger children, but there is some helpful dialog about the boys being angry, about not being able to cry, and the boys sharing special memories.

Make **snowmen**. Fold the arms of the snowman at his waist to allow a heart to be placed in his "hands". Each child will get a white snowman piece, 2 arms, a hat, a red nose, 3 cotton puffs, a scarf and a heart. Use Elmer's glue to glue on the cotton balls and glue sticks for everything else. The children can write a message on the heart and place it in the snowman's hands.

Children's Activity (A&B) #22:

*Read: <u>After Charlotte's Mom Died</u> by C. Spelman. This book has some good conversation topics. One thing this book addresses is that some people told Charlotte that death was a lot like sleep and she then became afraid of sleeping. She finds out later that this is not true and that she can sleep without being afraid of dying. She also talks about her fear of being an orphan.

In the book, the little girl **makes a wish**. Let the children think of a wish they have or a message that they might want to say to the one who died.

*Optional. Provide some **different puppets.** Have each child pick out a puppet and tell a story using the puppet (just like Charlotte did in the story). The story can be about something that has bothered them since the death or a story about a special memory that the puppet reminds them of.

Children's Activity (A&B) #23:
*Read: <u>The Brightest Star</u> by K.M.Hemery. This book is about a little girl whose mom died. A school assignment is to draw a picture of the family and the little girl struggles with drawing a picture without Mom. She talks to Dad and decides to draw a picture of something that reminds her of the special thing she and Dad did with Mom (look at the stars at the beach.)

Have the children **draw a picture** (like in the book) of a thing or favorite activity that reminds the child of the parent who died.

Children's Activity (A&B) #24:
*Read: <u>A Quilt for Elizabeth</u> by B.W. Tiffault. After her father's death, Elizabeth's grandmother helps her create a memory quilt, complete with her Dad's shirt pocket. This is a book of hopeful stories and tears.

As a family, make a **quilt** square including photos, items, and words that remind the family of their loved one.

Preteen Activities (Ages 9 - 12)

Preteen Opening (A) Activities

Preteen Activity #1A:

Play a game called **"Ask or Tell."** To play the game, the group sits in a circle. Someone starts the game by tossing a heart pillow, a stuffed animal or talking stick to another pre-teen. The preteen who receives the pillow chooses to "ask" or "tell." If he chooses to "ask," he asks a question to the one who tossed him the pillow. He could ask about the death in the family, or about the person who died, or about the preteen's feelings or thoughts about the death. Some examples of asking questions could be: *What was your favorite thing to do with your loved one? *What bothers you the most when you think about the death? *Where were you when your loved one died? *Do you ever feel angry about the death? *How has the death affected your relationship with your mom, dad, sister, brother? The preteen could also choose to "tell" some information about the death in his family. Some examples of "telling" could be: *I wish I could have told my loved one that I loved her before she died. *Since my father died, sometimes I feel pressured to act stronger than I feel. *Sometimes I find it hard to sleep at night because I start thinking about my dad. After the player "asks or tells," he tosses the pillow to another player. It is helpful for the facilitators to model the game first.

Preteen Activity #2A:

Give each pre-teen 2 or 3 **pipe cleaners**. Have them bend the pipe cleaners into something that reminds them of the person who died.

Preteen Activity #3A:

Use a piece of a clothesline **rope** and tie a knot for each preteen in your group. As they untie the knot have the preteens talk about something that has made them angry since the death (or any other topic that you feel would benefit your group). They have to keep talking as long as it takes to untie the knot. (Make the knots tight, but not impossible to untie.) If there are 10 preteens in the group, tie 10 knots in the rope. This sounds silly, but this activity can be very effective in helping the preteens talk about difficult topics.

Preteen Activity #4A:

Make a **feeling cube**. Take a block of wood and tape feeling words on the sides of the cube. Have the preteen roll the cube and tell of a time when he/she felt the feeling that shows on top of the cube. Continue as many times as is helpful. Possible feeling words: worried, happy, afraid, angry, alone, guilty, if only, and sad.

Preteen Activity #5A:

Pass out a **balloon** to each preteen. It would be helpful for a facilitator to model this activity first. Take the balloon and for each **blow** into the balloon the preteen tells something that has bothered him, angered him, hurt him, or changed for him since the death. When the balloon is full of air, let it go and it will "fly" around the room.

Preteen Activity #6A:

Pass around a **ball of yarn** and have each preteen cut a piece of yarn that represents how long they think their grieving will be. Discuss. Then, have the preteens lay the yarn on the floor and "graph" their grief showing the highs and lows of how it has been so far. Next, have the preteens use the yarn to show us what they think of their grief. For example, some preteens might stuff it in a pocket; others might wad it in a ball and stick it under a cushion where no one can see it; another might tie it to his shirt for all to see or possibly tie it in knots. What are some things that the group can come up with to show what they are experiencing in their grief?

Preteen Activity #7A:

Make or purchase **rocks** with the following words etched in the rocks: remember, hope, wonder and blessings. Place all four rocks in the middle of the room. Let the preteens pick a rock and share either a memory, a hope, something they wonder about (concerning the death or death in general), or a blessing in their lives.

Preteen Activity #8A:

Make a black velvet bag and fill it with "**feeling buttons.**" Each button (use pin-on type buttons) is a face depicting a different feeling. Pass around the bag and let each preteen pick a button. Then go around the group and have the preteen tell when they have felt the feeling that is on the button or how they relate to that feeling.

Preteen Activity #9A:

Make a **graffiti wall**. Place a large piece of butcher paper on the floor and make rectangles on the paper to represent bricks. Then give the preteens markers and let them write comments on the wall. These comments are generally things that have bothered the preteens since the death. This can open the door for a lot of issues that might be bothering the preteens: things people have said, things people have done that bothered them, ways they may have felt left out, or things that have made them angry.

Preteen Activity #10A:

Put together a **box of items**. This box should contain lots of items that preteens talk about when they remember their loved one: baseball, glasses, fishhook, telephone, cowboy hat, baseball cap, cross, hammer, apron, remote control, favorite sports team items, eyeglass case, airplane, playing cards, camera, baseball glove, aftershave, shin guards, tie, fish bobber, calculator, scrunchie, paintbrush, canteen, stethoscope, coffee mug, business card, keys, golf tee, newspaper, etc. Have the preteen pick out an item that reminds them of the person who died and tell why they think of their loved one when they see that object.

Preteen Activity #11A:

Have the preteens **interview** each other. Break the preteens into pairs. Have them all go to a separate place and ask each other the following questions. When they come back to the group they will tell the group what they found out about each other.
1. What has been the most difficult thing you have had to deal with since the death, so far?
2. What has been the most helpful thing that someone has said or done for you since the death?
3. Everyone expects you to feel sad. What is one feeling that you have experienced that you didn't expect to feel?
4. What is one thing that you have observed in yourself that you hadn't noticed before, or something that you have done that you didn't think you could do?

Activity #12A:

Make a **backpack of rocks** with feeling words painted on each rock. Place around 45 river rocks approximately 3" in diameter in this backpack. Have each preteen pick up and/or carry the backpack to see how heavy it is. The purpose of the feeling backpack is to give the pre-teens a tangible example of the weight of the feelings they have carried since their loved one died. As they recognize how difficult it is to carry the weight of their feelings, they can make choices as to what feelings to keep carrying. After each preteen has had the opportunity to feel the weight of the backpack, let the preteens examine the feeling rocks. To make the backpack lighter they can examine the rocks to determine which feelings they don't have, so they can discard those feelings. Ask them to discuss the feelings they are discarding. Ask other group members if they could discard those feelings. The preteen will then determine how many feelings they can choose to carry. Ask the preteen what is benefited by continuing to carry their chosen feelings, such as anger, guilt, resentment. Next, have the preteens brainstorm ways they can feel supported in carrying their feelings. Sharing feelings with friends and family or coming to a support group can be a method of sharing the 'burden' of carrying feelings. Have two preteens carry the backpack together to show how sharing the weight can make the load easier.

Preteen Activity #13A:

Play the **"Starburst"** game. Make four groups of colored cards that coordinate with the four flavors of the Starburst candies. Red cards=cherry, pink cards=strawberry, yellow cards=lemon and orange=orange. The preteen gets to eat a starburst candy that coordinates with the color card that the preteen answers. These cards include questions, topics, and opportunities to share memories. The game cards are included in the addendum.

Preteen Activity #14A:

Make two **soccer balls** with questions written on the open spaces of the ball. "Throw" a ball to a preteen and where his/her thumb lands is the question he/she is to answer. If both thumbs land on a question space, he can choose which question to answer. There are some spaces with "Wilson," etc. on the ball, so just tell the preteens to use the space closest to their thumb. After the preteen has answered his question, he throws it to another preteen. See addendum for list of questions.

Preteen Activity #15A:

Talk about **depression**. It is helpful for the preteens to know that this is a normal part of grieving. Have the preteens put together a group list of some physical and emotional things that they see in themselves as part of depression. Use a dry erase marker board/ chalkboard and make two columns (physical and emotional) and write down what the preteens come up with. Next, brainstorm some things they can do when they are feeling depressed. Some ideas: journal, call a friend, ride your bike, rollerblade, jog, play a video game, etc.

Preteen Activity #16A:

Start off with this **simple game**. The first person (start with facilitator to model for the preteens) says their name, who died, and their favorite thing to do with the person who died. The second person then says what the first person said, (name, who died, and favorite thing to do) and then tells their own info. The third person then says what the first and second person said and his own info and you go around the group constantly adding. This is a good get-to-know-each-other exercise as well as a way to share for the preteens.

Preteen Activity #17A:

Take a ball of yarn and when the ball of yarn is thrown to a pre-teen, he/she is to tell something that he/she is **concerned or worried** about. This can also be used as an **"up-date"** activity telling the group what is going on for that preteen. Facilitators should model this activity first. The first person holds the beginning end of the yarn, shares his concern and while still holding the yarn, throws the ball part of the yarn to someone on the other side of the group circle. That person tells his concern and holds the yarn and throws the ball of yarn to a new preteen. The idea is to create a "web" in the middle of the group from passing the ball of yarn back and forth with each person still holding on to their part of the yarn. After everyone has had a chance to share, starting with the end of the yarn, go back and roll up the ball of yarn sharing a positive thing in the preteen's life.

Preteen Activity #18A:

Place 30 **miscellaneous items** on a tray. Keep the tray covered. Gather the group around the tray. When you have everyone's attention, lift off the cover and give the group 10 seconds to look at the items. Then cover the tray and give each preteen a piece of paper and have them list as many items as they can remember. After everyone has finished, see how many everyone listed. Next, have the group compile a list of the items. Have a facilitator write down the items the group remembers. You will find that the group remembers more of the items than the individuals. Ask the group, "What did this teach us?" The answer hopefully is that what was difficult to do alone, is easier with others. Relate this to grieving. Isn't it easier when you talk to others rather than holding it in and trying to deal with this alone?

Preteen Activity #19A:

Go around the room and ask each preteen what **date(s)** are coming up that he/she is worried about: birthday, anniversary of death, holiday, etc. Then discuss what they can do to help them cope with that day. Some suggestions: letting friends and family know that this is a difficult day for them and not assume everyone will know; discuss with family members and plan a special thing to do on that difficult day, this plan can include remembering the person who died if they choose, or just a special thing to do to make the day better; write down how he/she is feeling; or use other suggestions from the preteens who have already passed some of those difficult days.

Preteen Activity #20A:

Make a **handout of feeling words**. The words are to be arranged diagonally, vertically and horizontally. Have the preteens circle the feelings they have felt and cross out the feelings that they haven't felt. Separate into small groups and discuss. Words used are angry, abandonment, numb, relieved, indecisive, envious, suffering, inferior, lonely, outraged, disgusted, beaten, suicidal, lost, happy, fear, darkness, failure, grief-stricken, shock, overwhelmed, pain, unknown, frightened, rejection, looking foolish, success, full of self-hatred and good.

Preteen Activity #21A:

Give the preteens an assignment to bring in a **special possession or memento** that reminds them of the person who died, a special possession that the loved one gave them, or a possession that was important to the loved one. Let each preteen have the opportunity to tell the story of the significance of the item. Next, using a Polaroid camera, take a close-up photo of each preteen holding their special possession. Then place this special photo in a photo holder/folder. The preteen can decorate this photo folder as they wish.

Preteen Activity #22A:

Give the preteens an assignment to find a person (friend, co-worker, or relative of the deceased) that can **tell the preteen a story** about the person who died — something that the preteen didn't know. When the preteens come to group, have them share the new information they have found out about their loved one. How did they feel to find out something new?

Preteen Activity #23A:

Complete the sentence: The **most helpful** thing anyone has said to me to help me cope with my grief is ...

Preteen Activity #24A:

Using a **stretchy cord,** two facilitators each hold an end stretching the cord tightly. On one end have a clothespin with a picture of a smiley face and on the other end have a clothespin with a picture of a sad face. The smiley face represents the preteen feeling wonderful, great, etc. and the sad face represents the preteen feeling horrible, terrible, or very sad. One by one the preteens will place a clothespin on the cord, representing where on the line they are feeling tonight. In the middle, for example would be some good, some bad. Have the preteen explain why they placed their clothespin where they did. If you want, you can take a piece of paper and clothespin everyone's name on the cord. You may substitute an angry face or a guilty face if these are topics that your group would benefit discussing.

Preteen Activity #25A:

Make up a sheet of paper with four rows of five puzzle pieces each for a total of 20 **puzzle pieces** on the paper. Make it look like a jigsaw puzzle. On the outside pieces, have the preteen write something in each puzzle piece that describes him (things he likes to do, words that describe him, activities, etc). On the inside puzzle pieces, have the preteen write things that he has had to cope with since the death, some things that bother him, some feelings he has experienced or possibly some things that he misses doing with his loved one. After everyone has finished, give each preteen a different colored marker. Next the preteens will pass around their sheets. If another preteen has a similar interest or has also experienced the same thing shown on the puzzle page, the preteen makes a mark on that puzzle piece with his colored marker. After everyone has looked at the sheets, the preteens all get their own sheets back and find that others in the group have similar interests and experiences. Discuss. Are there some things they saw on others' sheets that they wish they had included on their own sheets? Were there some things that they have not experienced but a lot of others have experienced?

Preteen Activity #1B:

This activity is helpful for memories and anger. Have the preteens draw on **pillowcases**. On one side, have the preteen draw all the happy memories that they can remember of their loved one. On the other side, draw all the things that have made them angry about the death. Make sure the preteens use permanent fabric markers. Put a paper bag inside the pillowcase so that the colors do not go on to the other side. Explain to the preteens that when they get home, they should put their pillow in this pillowcase. When they are angry, hit the bed with the angry side of the pillowcase. Then at night, to have happy thoughts, sleep with the memory side up. On the hem of the "happy" side of the pillowcase the preteens could autograph each other's pillowcase, if they so choose.

Preteen Activity #2B:

Give each preteen a large piece of manila paper. Divide in fourths. In one section the preteen will write his/her name vertically. Then for each letter, the preteen is to write an **adjective** that describes him/her. For example if the preteen's name is Bill, he might write "basketball" for B, "intelligent" for I, "likable" for L, and "lively" for L. In the second section they will do this same activity, except using the loved one's name. The next two sections are to be collage activities, with one being a collage of things that describe the preteen, and the other a **collage** of things that describe the loved one who died. Share in groups.

Preteen Activity #3B:

Make **memory boxes**. These are to be used to place a special item that the loved one who died may have given the preteens, or mementos of special times, or this could be a place to put notes or drawings to the deceased. Pass out a cigar box or cardboard pencil box to each preteen. Then have the preteens cut out words and pictures from magazines that remind them of their loved one. Glue these pictures and words on the box, encouraging the preteens to cover the box entirely. The idea is to have the entire box covered so that they don't see the box. When finished, using sponge brushes, have the preteens cover the box with Modge Podge. This adds a shiny finish to the box and finishes it off nicely. Supplies: box, glue, Modge Podge, brushes, magazines, scissors, and paper bags to work on.

Preteen Activity #4B:

Have the preteens **draw** a picture.
Some suggested topics are:
*   A special memory
*   How it feels to have lost a parent or other loved one (brother, sister, etc.)
*   What death looks like to them
*   Give each preteen a large piece of manila paper. Draw a line down the middle of the page. On one side the preteens can draw a picture of the family before the death and on the other side a picture of the family after the death. These can be "then" and "now" or "before" and "after" drawings. Encourage the preteens to draw what comes to mind for them. It could be a picture of what the family looks like or a special memory or event that happened before and after the death.

- Have the preteen either draw a picture or write a description of the person who died. Have them do this as if they were describing this person to someone who knows nothing about the person who died. They could include a detailed physical description and detailed information about what the person liked to do, hobbies, interests, occupation, what was fun for that person, and some descriptive words that describe the person's personality.

Preteen Activity #5B:

Make **memory bracelets.** Give each preteen a 12" piece of elastic thread which is available in white, black, gold, and silver. Spread out on trays a wide variety of beads of different colors, shapes (include hearts) and letters. Have the preteens pick out beads that represent a special memory or detail about the person who died. Some ideas are: white bead for a golfer, orange bead for a basketball fan, 4 black beads for tire salesman, blue and gray for Dallas Cowboy fan, red, white and blue for a special 4th of July memory or military person, and the red heart bead for love for the person who died, etc. The preteens can use the letters for the name or initials of the loved one. Brainstorm some other suggestions to get the preteens thinking of how these beads could represent the person who died. Tie a bead onto one end of the piece of thread so that the other beads do not fall off. Once the beads are strung, tie the two ends together so that it fits fairly snug around the wrist. Cut off the extra thread. Next, pass out paper and have the preteens write the significance of each bead. When everyone is finished, place all of the bracelets in the middle of the group. Discuss how different all the bracelets are and that we are all different with our own individual sets of memories. Then, one by one, have the preteens explain the meaning of their memory bracelet.

Preteen Activity #6B:

Make a **memory necklace/key chain/gym bag tag/or zipper pull.** First the preteens will cut words describing their loved one from magazines. They may also want to cut out letters to write their loved one's name. Then, using a glue stick, attach each word to a separate colored index card, leaving an inch at one end for a hole. Trim the tags leaving a border around the words. Take clear packing tape and cover the word/index cards. Trim excess tape. Punch a hole in the end of each word/index card and thread a small piece of yarn. Attach all of the words to either a yarn chain or a silver circle. The preteens can use the yarn chain to make a necklace, or by using the silver circle they can make a key chain, a gym bag tag, or a zipper pull.

Preteen Activity #7B:

Make a **secret thoughts pouch.** This is a special pouch to keep in a private place to help keep the preteen's private thoughts. Using two pieces of stiff paper, punch holes around the edges using a hole punch. Then use yarn to lace the pieces of paper together. After the preteens have made (and decorated) their pouches, they can write or draw their secret thoughts on a piece of paper and hide it in the pouch. They could write things that make them mad, things that people have said, write or draw something for the person who died, write things they didn't get a chance to say, or write things that they are worried about. When they get home, they need to find a place where they can hide their memory pouch. They can add to their memory pouch at any time. Supplies needed: 2 pieces of stiff paper approximately 6" x 8", hole punch, yarn, little pieces of paper (for secret thoughts/pictures), and magic markers.

Preteen Activity #8B:

Make a **"message in a bottle."** Each preteen will get a decorative bottle to paint. Then the preteen will write a message to the person who died and place it in this bottle. This message can be something they didn't get a chance to say, a regret, or an update on how their life is without their loved one. Encourage the preteens to add to this bottle when they want to relay a message or think of something else they need to say to their loved one.

Supplies: each preteen gets a glass bottle, special paints for glass, paintbrushes, special markers for glass, parchment paper (to write message on), and ribbon (to tie to message and place in bottle.)

Preteen Activity #9B:

Discuss the idea of **"mending a broken heart."** Some thoughts on this topic can include: Is the heart broken? Can we have a new normal heart? Can you live without a heart? Can you start over with the pieces you have? Do you have to grow a new one?

Supplies needed: red and white construction paper, glue, pens, markers, scissors, magazines. First, have the preteens cut out a red heart. Decorate the heart with words that describe how they are feeling and add some pictures from magazines that describe the feelings they are experiencing. They may also choose to decorate the heart with pictures or feeling words about their loved one. Once they have completed the heart, have the preteens rip it up (not telling them why). Next, have the preteens put the heart back together, gluing on a white piece of paper. Discuss what this new heart looks like. Some comments may include: it is a new heart, has holes in it, the edges don't meet anymore etc.

Preteen Activity #10B:

Give each preteen a smooth, 3" river rock or shell and using acrylic paints, have them **paint a** rock or shell for their loved one. Place the rock/shells in a special place at your agency (around a special tree, in a memorial garden, etc.) The preteens can write a message, or paint a picture of an item that reminds the preteen of the loved one. After the rock is painted, a facilitator should spray the rocks with the fixative spray. If dry before the preteens leave, lay the rocks around the special place as the preteen says their loved one's name.

Preteen Activity #11B:

Make a handout titled **"Changes, changes, changes."** Divide the page in half; on one half have the preteens list changes in their family; on the other half list changes in themselves. Then write subcategories as: changes in the past year, possible changes for the next year, and changes I would like to make now.

Preteen Activity #12B:

Make a **collage,** individually or as a group. Cut out pictures from a magazine of things we learned from the person who died, things that remind us of the person who died, and/or things that show how we have felt since our loved one died. These pictures can be glued on a poster board if done as a group or on a separate piece of paper if done individually. Encourage sharing of the collages.

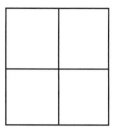

Preteen Activity #13B:

Give each preteen a piece of paper and divide it into squares, one square for each **family member** including themselves. In that square have the preteen write feelings or actions they have observed in each family member (self included). Another option for this activity is to have a square for each family member (including the deceased) and write what each person has lost since the death. Then notice things they have seen in one family member that they may not have seen in another (or in themselves). Discuss similarities and differences with the group members.

Preteen Activity #14B:

This is a helpful activity if your preteen group meets at the same time as your adult group. As a group, have the preteens make a **list of things that the adults** in the adult room should know about grieving preteens. This list could be given to the adult room to discuss, and to become aware of the concerns/problems that the preteens are experiencing that the adults may be ignoring or may not be aware of. These should be anonymous, no preteen names given. An example of the comments the preteens want to pass on is finding a way for the family to discuss their grief, and not protecting the kids by not talking about it.

Preteen Activity #15B:

Have the preteens write a **question, problem, or concern** (anonymously) that they would like the group to discuss or role play. Put the pieces of paper in a basket and take them out one by one and have the group discuss or act out a solution. These can be questions concerning how to deal with friends, family, classmates, or any problems they are currently worried about or experiencing since the death.

Preteen Activity #16B:

Make a **visual display of facial expressions** of the different feelings that people might have when grieving. Have each preteen think of a feeling he/she has felt since the death and using a Polaroid camera, take his/her picture showing that expression. Have the group display the feeling pictures on a poster board for others to see.

Preteen Activity #17B:

This activity is to help the preteens discuss things that worry or concern them. Have the preteens make a **worry balloon** that the preteens can take out and squeeze when they are worried. As they make their worry balloon, encourage a discussion of the things that worry/concern the preteens. Supplies needed: 2 balloons per preteen, salt or flour, funnel, pencil, and a large sheet of paper or paper bag. Pass out two balloons and a pencil to each preteen. Inflate one balloon slightly. Put a pencil in the second balloon. Next slip the second balloon with the pencil into the first balloon. Then take out the pencil. This is to make the balloon a double thickness so that we don't need to worry about the balloon breaking. For this next step, have the preteens work on a piece of paper or a paper bag. The preteens need to work in pairs, and help each other fill the balloon with salt or flour using the funnel. Once the balloons are filled, tie a knot in the balloon. Let the preteens squeeze and knead the balloon. Tell the preteens that they can get these out and knead anytime they have a worry or concern.

Preteen Activity #18B:

Balloon launch. Give each preteen a helium balloon and a tag with a string. Let each preteen write a message on the tag and then tie it to the balloon. As a group, go outside and "launch" the balloons together and watch them as they go into the sky. This can be used for special occasions or on special days like birthdays and anniversaries.

Preteen Activity #19B:

Make a **memory page** about the loved one who died. Possible topics to include are name, birthday, date of death, favorite food, favorite fun thing to do, words to describe loved one, things he/she was best at, favorite memory, "I remember you when ...," "I feel closer to you when ... ."

Preteen Activity #20B:

When a new preteen comes to your group, give him/her a **journal book** to write/draw about special memories. For this age group I recommend "Memories Live Forever." Encourage them to add photographs and mementos to this special book. It can be helpful for the preteen to ask the adults in his life to also add to this journal book.

Preteen Combined A and B Activities

Preteen Activity (A&B) #1:

Discuss the **funeral**. It might be best for a facilitator to share about the funeral or memorial service for his/her loved one first. Share things such as what it was like, how you felt, etc. Was it in a church, pretty house, or funeral home? Was the ceremony a special way to say goodbye? How did you feel about the ceremony afterwards? Did you have any input in what happened at the ceremony? Be sure to give each person an opportunity to share if they choose to.

Have the preteens share their loved one's **obituary**, or **design a tombstone** for their loved one, including some thoughts and feelings that they would want people to know about their loved one.

Preteen Activity (A&B) #2:

Give the preteens a homework assignment to bring in a **song** that they have found to be helpful, or perhaps the favorite song of the deceased, or a song that reminds them of their loved one. Give each preteen an opportunity to share their song and tell how they feel when they hear it. What words or phrases affect them? Also have available the following songs if some have forgotten to bring in something:

- The Dance by Garth Brooks
- One Sweet Day by Mariah Carey and Boyz II Men
- The Living Years by Mike and the Mechanics
- It's So Hard to Say Goodbye to Yesterday by Boyz II Men
- Once in a While by Billy Dean

The preteens will **make a CD** representative of their loved ones. Provide each preteen with two squares of paper that will fit inside a CD case. You can purchase blank CD cases for this purpose. On the first square the preteen can draw a picture of the loved one or a picture of a special memory or something representative of the loved one. This drawing is supposed to be like the front of a CD. On the second square the preteen makes a list of song titles that could be representative of the loved one. These can be real song titles or the preteens can make up titles for songs. For example, for a loved one who liked baseball a song title might include Take Me Out to the Ballgame. Have available some sample CDs for ideas. When everyone is finished, share the CDs and discuss music and how songs affect the preteens.

Preteen Activity (A&B) #3:

*Read: Poem "I Am." Using the same words as in the poem, have the preteens complete their own "I Am" poem.

"I Am" by Keli Klecher	"I Am"
I **Am** a daughter who misses her father.	I Am ...
I **Wonder** if I will ever see him again.	I Wonder ...
I **Hear** his voice wherever I am.	I Hear ...
I **See** him in all of my dreams.	I See ...
I **Want** to meet him again someday.	I Want ...
I **Am** a daughter who misses her father.	I Am ...
I **Pretend** I am with him everyday.	I Pretend ...
I **Feel** happy when I see him in my dreams.	I Feel ...
I **Touch** his grave on the holidays.	I Touch ...
I **Cry** when somebody says something about him.	I Cry ...
I **Am** a daughter who misses her father.	I Am ...
I **Understand** I will not see him for awhile.	I Understand ...
I **Say** I would give my life to see him again.	I Say ...
I **Dream** of him everyday.	I Dream ...
I **Try** to touch him in my dreams.	I Try ...
I **Hope** to see him again someday.	I Hope ...
I **Am** a daughter who misses her father.	I Am ...

Preteen Activity (A&B) #4:

First let's talk about wearing **masks** during grief. Who sees themselves putting on a mask, or notices the parent or other family members wearing a mask? Do they need to wear a mask when they come to this support group? Is this a place where for a short while they can attempt to take off the mask? What would happen if they let people see how they are really feeling? What does wearing the mask feel like?

Provide papiermaché **masks** for the preteens to paint. This is a two-meeting project because you paint the inside at one session and the outside at the second session. The preteens can pick which side they want to paint first. The idea is that the outside is what we show the world. This can be what the preteen looks like, including the feelings they show, or they can be really creative and make it a representation of who they are to the world (plays sports, is in the band, dances, likes Country-Western, etc.). The inside of the mask portrays what they feel inside. This can be expressed in words (alone, wounded, sad, angry, devastated) or painting how they feel. This is an opportunity to be really creative. Another option might be to have some choose to make the mask to represent what death looks like.
Supplies: papiermaché masks, a wide variety of paints, brushes, and markers.

Preteen Activity (A&B) #5:

Start off with the opening topic of **returning to school** after the death. Was this difficult for the preteens? What is different for them (relating to school) now that the loved has died? Some preteens are possibly home alone now, or the parent who used to always pick them up doesn't pick them up anymore, or there's no one to make sure they get to school, or will help with homework.

Some of the preteens have mentioned that classmates/friends have made negative/hurtful comments to them. Discuss that so many times people (adults included) say things that hurt even though the people may have meant well. Have the preteens share some situations where they were uncomfortable because of some things people said and brainstorm some responses to say if the situation arises again. Ask the preteens what they wish people had done or not done, or said or not said to them after the death. Have the group make up a **handout** for newly bereaved preteens that they wish they would have received after their loved one's death. What would you tell them about the grieving process?

Preteen Activity (A&B) #6:

Use a dry erase/chalkboard board and make a **group list of things** (people, situations) that have made the preteens angry since the death. Examples: "I hate it when my friends say they know exactly how I feel and they haven't had a parent die," "I wish my sister/brother didn't try to be my parent." "I wish I didn't feel like I had to be perfect because my sibling died." "I'm angry that no one told me that my mother was dying." "I'm angry that I didn't get to pick out anything for the funeral".

Optional: The preteens are going to make a **"button heart,"** which they can keep with them in their pocket or their backpack. They can push the button whenever they feel themselves getting angry. It will help them focus on why they are angry and hopefully dispel some of the anger. Have preteens choose two fabric hearts and a button that reminds them of their loved one. Have them glue the button onto one of the hearts. They can decorate the hearts with fabric markers if they choose. Glue the hearts almost together. Leave room to stuff with a little quilt batting. Then finish gluing hearts together. Remind preteens that when they push their button, they can think of their loved one, count to ten, hold their breath or do whatever works for them. (Brainstorm ideas.)

Provide some **activities** to help the preteens express their anger. Let the preteens pick which activities they would like to do.

- Let the preteens write who/what makes them angry on a piece of paper, then tape that paper to a soda can. They can squish or stomp on the can with their feet.
- Give each preteen a phone book and let them rip it up.
- Give each preteen a cup of ice cubes and let the preteen throw them on the ground or at a wall.

CHILDREN are so often the forgotten mourners and I believe strongly that they can experience hope and healing when they have the opportunity to grieve in the supporting presence of others who share the same pain.

— *Gay McWhorter*

Teen Activities (Ages 13 - 18)

Teen Opening (A) Activities

Teen Activity #1A:
Topic: What has changed for you since your (parent, sibling, friend, grandparent) died?

Teen Activity #2A:
Topic: How has the family changed since the death?

Teen Activity #3A:
Topic: Is there an event, activity, or "day" that is looming ahead that you are dreading, knowing it will be a difficult day or event without your loved one? We have found that the first date, prom, graduation, getting a driver's license, getting married are just a few of the events that teens worry about. It is helpful to discuss with teens some coping strategies to help them with these days. Sometimes it is helpful for the teen to bring an item of the deceased to the event (such as graduation). It can also be helpful to take a special memento from the special event to the cemetery following the event. It is also helpful for the teen to consider if there is a person in his/her life that can help him cope with the special date and to ask that person for help. We cannot assume others will know that this is a difficult date for us.

Teen Activity #4A:
Topic: How has the death changed you and the way you want to live your life? Is there a change in you that you do not like? Is there a change in you that you do like?

Teen Activity #5A:
Topic: Are there changes at home that are difficult for you to handle? One of the issues teens talk about following the death of a parent is the issue of the surviving parent dating. Some concerns teens tell us are: Does this mean the parent doesn't love the parent who died anymore? How will this change affect their lives? Will the teens have to take on more responsibilities with younger siblings? Will the parent still have time for them?

Teen Activity #6A:
Topic: Where were you when you learned of the death?

Teen Activity #7A:
Topic: Tell about the last time you were with the person who died.

Teen Activity #8A:
Topic: In what way has your relationship with your friends or family members changed as a result of the death?

Teen Activity #9A:
Topic: In some families, the death and our feelings about the death are not discussed. Some use the analogy that there is "an elephant in the room" or "a dead horse on the dining room table." It is big, it stinks, and everyone sees it, but everyone acts as though it isn't there. How does your family deal with the death? Is it a dead horse on the table, or do you openly discuss it, or is it somewhere in the middle?

Teen Activity #10A:
Topic: What are some things people have said or done (or not done) that have not been helpful since the death?

Teen Activity #11A:
Topic: Share a good thing and a bad (difficult) thing that has happened since we last met.

Teen Activity #12A:
Topic: Did you get a chance to say goodbye to the person who died? If not, what would you have liked to say?

Teen Activity #13A:
Topic: What special gift or legacy did your loved one leave you? This is not a discussion about a possession, but a special quality about the person who died that the teen would want to cherish and incorporate into their own lives. Was there a special thing that the person who died did that impacted the teen's life?

Teen Activity #14A:
Topic: Discuss dreams and nightmares. Has anyone had trouble sleeping?

Teen Activity #15A:
Topic: Use a marker board and compile a list of good (effective) and bad (ineffective) coping skills. Many teens turn to drinking and drugs to escape from grief. Have the teens add to these lists and discuss both modes of coping behaviors.

Teen Activity #16A:

Topic: Discuss what the teens thought about death prior to their loved one's death. Next, discuss how they feel about death now that they have had a loved one die. Do they find that they are more aware of deaths in their school and in the news? Discuss also about how death is portrayed in movies and television. Do the teens find that they think of death more now? Do they think of their own death? Other loved one's deaths?

Teen Activity #17A:

Make and pass out a copy of "Grief," pages 6-10 from the book, <u>Straight Talk About Death for Teenagers</u> by Earl Grollman. Discuss.

Teen Activity #18A:

Make and pass out a copy of "Death of a Parent," pages 43-47 from the book, <u>Straight Talk About Death for Teenagers</u> by Earl Grollman. Discuss.

Teen Activity #19A:

Make and pass out a copy of "Death of a Sibling," pages 49-52 from the book, <u>Straight Talk About Death for Teenagers</u> by Earl Grollman. Discuss.

Teen Activity #20A:

Make and pass out a copy of "Accepting the Pain," pages 93-95 from the book, <u>Straight Talk About Death for Teenagers</u> by Earl Grollman. Discuss.

Teen Activity #21A:

Make and pass out a copy of "Lengthening Grief Through Harmful Shortcuts: Drugs and Drinking," pages 96-97 from the book, <u>Straight Talk About Death for Teenagers</u> by Earl Grollman. Discuss.

Teen Activity #22A:

Make and pass out a copy of "Talking," pages 101-103 from the book, <u>Straight Talk About Death for Teenagers</u> by Earl Grollman. Discuss.

Teen Activity #23A:

Make and pass out a copy of "Getting over It," pages 123-124 from the book, <u>Straight Talk About Death for Teenagers</u> by Earl Grollman. Discuss.

Teen Activity #24A:

Music: Play the song, "How Can I Help You Say Goodbye?" by Reba McIntire. Some possible discussion topics from this song: Life involves changes (good and bad); changes sometimes involve choices and you can choose to survive or choose not to survive; it's OK to hurt when things happen; and memories help when you have to say goodbye.

Teen Activity #25A:

Music: Play the song, "One More Day" by Diamond Rio. This song talks about how we always want one more day with someone who has died.

Teen Activity #26A:

Music: Play the song, "Everybody Hurts" by REM. This song talks about how "everybody hurts, everybody cries." Discuss the topic: Can teens cry and allow themselves to grieve?

Teen Activity #27A:

Music: Play the song, "One Sweet Day" by Boyz ll Men. Discuss.

Teen Activity #28A:

Music: Play the song, "Tears in Heaven" by Eric Clapton. Discuss.

Teen Activity #29A:

Music: Play the song, "Nobody Knows" by The Tony Rich Project. Discuss.

Teen Activity #30A:

Music: Play the song, "It's So Hard to Say Goodbye to Yesterday" by Boyz II Men. Discuss.

Teen Activity #31A:

Music: Play the song, "Once in a While" by Billy Dean. Discuss.

Teen Activity #32A:

Music: Play the song, "If I Had Only Known" by Reba McIntire. Discuss.

Teen Activity #33A:

Have the teens bring in a **photo** of the deceased, a **possession** that belonged to the deceased, or a special possession that the deceased gave to the teen. Allow the teen to share the item or photo that he/she has brought to group.

Teen Activity #34A:

Activity #1: Using a marker board, make **four columns** with one of the following headings in each column: Feelings of Grief, Behaviors of Grief, Physical Reactions to Grief, and Thoughts of Grief. Have the group share ways they have experienced each of these categories.

Teen Activity #35A:

Have the group stand in a circle and using only two fingers, balance a **hula hoop**. There are only two rules: the teens must maintain contact with the hula hoop using only the two fingers and the teens are to lower the hula hoop to the ground. Note: even though the hula hoop is supposed to go down, it always rises since everyone is concentrating on establishing contact with the hula hoop. The group finds that there needs to be teamwork to make the hula hoop go down. It is helpful to tie this exercise into the importance of being part of a group dealing with a difficult topic like death. After a death, we can't do it all alone. We need to reach out to people, even though it may be against our nature to do so. It is also a helpful exercise to discuss who we can turn to for support.

Teen Activity #36A:

Do a **human knot activity**. Have the teens stand in a circle. Each teen takes the hand of another teen that is across from them in the circle. Then, not letting go, they need to un-knot themselves until they are in a circle again. (The teens will find that some teens may be backwards and they may need to step over hands, etc. to un-knot themselves.) Next discuss what the teens learned from this activity. Hint: working together helps because we all started off tangled up and things appeared impossible, but we can straighten things out and we don't always end up the way we think we will be.

Teen Activity #37A:

Compile a **rock and shell basket** filled with all types of rocks and shells with different types of surfaces and edges: smooth, rough, sharp, smooth and sharp, broken, coiled, etc. Have the teen pick a rock or shell that describes how they are feeling tonight and tell why they picked that particular rock or shell.

Teen Activity #38A:

For many who are grieving it is important to **tell their story** many times to different people until it begins to feel like it really happened. Give each teen an opportunity to tell their story. Some details they may want to include are: What were they doing the day of the death? What happened? What was their initial reaction? How did other people react? It might be helpful for the facilitator to tell his/her story first.

Teen Activity #39A:

As a group, make an anonymous **list of things that the teens want the adults in their lives to know** about grieving teens. *(See Preteen Activity #14B.)*

Teen Activity #40A:
Play a game called **"Ask or Tell."** *(See Preteen Activity #1A.)*

Teen Activity #41A:
Use the **feeling cube**. *(See Preteen Activity #4A.)*

Teen Activity #42A:
Use the **balloon** blow activity. *(See Preteen Activity #5A.)*

Teen Activity #43A:
Use the **ball of yarn** activity. *(See Preteen Activity #6A.)*

Teen Activity #44A:
Use the **four rocks** activity. *(See Preteen Activity #7A.)*

Teen Activity #45A:
Use the **graffiti wall** activity. *(See Preteen Activity #9A.)*

Teen Activity #46A:
Use the **interview** activity. *(See Preteen Activity #11A.)*

Teen Activity #47A:
Use the **backpack of rocks** activity. *(See Preteen Activity #12A.)*

Teen Activity #48A:
Play the **"Starburst"** game. *(See Preteen Activity #13A.)*

Teen Activity #49A:
Use a **ball of yarn** as an update activity. *(See Preteen Activity #17A.)*

Teen Activity #50A:
Use the **handout of feeling words**. *(See Preteen Activity #20A.)*

Teen Activity #51A:
Use the **box of items**. *(See Preteen Activity #10A.)*

Teen Activity #52A:
Make up a sheet of paper with four rows of five puzzle pieces each for a total of 20 **puzzle pieces** on the paper (make it look like a jigsaw puzzle). *(See Preteen Activity #25A.)*

Teen Main (B) Activities

Teen Activity #1B:

Make **timelines**. Pass out paper and pencils to the teens and have them draw a horizontal line on the paper. The teens next will note important life events on the line, writing their approximate age at the time the event occurred. If the teen perceived the event as positive, they will write it above the line; if the teen perceived the event as negative, they will write it below the line. Encourage the teens to also look to the future and write what they hope will occur in their future.

Teen Activity #2B:

The paper bag activity. Pass out a brown paper lunch bag to each teen. On the outside the teen is to draw and/or write special characteristics, hobbies, and "words" that describe either the deceased or themselves. Next, the teens will write on small pieces of paper topics or issues that they have struggled with since the death. These can also be some things that are difficult for the teen to discuss. Have the teens put these small pieces of paper into their paper bag. Ask if any teen might be willing to share one of the items in their bag for the group to discuss.

Teen Activity #3B:

I call this activity the **rock to survive**. Give each teen a river rock (approximately 3"). On this rock, using permanent markers (white and silver work well on the river rocks) have the teen write a word or words that describe what they think a teen needs to survive the death of a loved one. Some examples of words the teens have given us are: courage, humor, faith, friends, and talking to people. Discuss. Place these rocks in a special basket in your teen group room so that new teens coming to your group can see what has helped other teens to survive the death.

Teen Activity #4B:

Play the **grief game**. Using a large poster board, make a game board with questions for the teens to answer. The teens each have a game piece and the teens move their game piece by rolling a die and answering the questions on the board. These questions are included in the addendum.

Teen Activity #5B:

This is a revision of the preteen backpack activity for use as an additional activity for a teen group. *(See Preteen Activity #12A for a complete description of the backpack activity.)* Use the same rocks with feeling words painted on the rocks from the preteen backpack activity. Have one person hold a lunch type paper bag and one by one add a rock to the bag, commenting on the feeling word on the rock as the teen adds the rock to the bag. Keep adding rocks until the bag rips. Next compare this activity to our grief: if we continue to stuff our grief, something is going to fall apart and it can exhibit in our life as a physical, emotional or behavior problem.

Teen Activity #6B:

Take a **Jenga game** and make it into a grief game. The Jenga game is a wooden block game that can be purchased at a toy store. The game has 54 wood pieces and we have written questions on half of these wood blocks. See the addendum for the list of questions. The teens stack the blocks in an 18-story tower using the instructions given in the game package. The game is played by removing a block from the stack without causing the tower to fall. When the teen removes a block with a question written on it, he/she must answer that question. The game ends when the tower falls.

Teen Activity #7B:

Have the teens make believe that they can get into a **time machine** and go back in time. Have the teens think of a day or date that they would go back to and change one thing if they could. What would that change be? Or can they think of one day or date they would like to relive again?

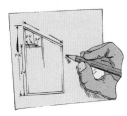

Teen Activity #8B:

Give each teen a piece of paper and pencil. Have them draw a **floor plan** of their house, in simple terms, showing the bedrooms, kitchen, bathroom, family room, front yard, back yard, etc. Then have the teens think of things in each of these rooms that remind them of the person who died. These could be things that are still in the rooms as well as things that used to be in the rooms. For example, in the family room the remote control might remind the teen of the person who died, in the kitchen it could be the place where the loved one sat, in the bathroom it could be the colognes that used to be on the counter, etc. If the teen has moved since the death, have the teen think of the last place they lived with their loved one or things that are in their current home. If the teen and the loved one did not live in the same home, have the teen draw the home (or place) where they spent the most time with their loved one.

Teen Activity #9B:

Give each teen a 4" x 4" ceramic white tile. Using permanent markers, have the teens **decorate the tile** in memory of the person who died. Many teens have used this activity to write a message or draw a picture of something that reminds them of the person who died. Prior to the teens decorating the tiles, they must first be treated with a glass/tile preparation substance. After they are decorated spray two coats of fixative spray on the tiles. These tiles can be added to a wall in your agency or you could add felt to the back of the tile and let the teen take the tile home.

Teen Activity #10B:

Have the teens write a **letter** to the person who died. Some possible topics: Things they miss doing now that the loved one has died. Something they wish they had said or not said. Something they wish the deceased had said or not said. Something they wish they had done or not done. Something they want the deceased to know about. Something they cherish about the time they had together.

Teen Activity #11B:

Using **candles** can set a mood in your group that encourages discussion. Use a large glass hurricane lamp and using special glass markers, have each teen write his/her loved one's name on the lamp. Place this hurricane lamp over a large lighted pillar candle and shut off the lights.

Teen Activity #12B:

Make a **memory page** about the loved one who died. *(See Preteen Activity #19B.)*

Teen Activity #13B:

Balloon launch. *(See Preteen Activity #18B.)*

Teen Activity #14B:

Have the teens **draw** a picture. *(See Preteen Activity #4B for a list of picture topics.)*

Teen Activity #15B:

Make a **worry balloon**. *(See Preteen Activity #17B.)*

Teen Activity #16B:
Have the teens write a **question, problem, or a concern** (anonymously) that they would like the group to discuss or role play. *(See Preteen Activity #15B.)*

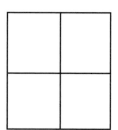

Teen Activity #17B:
Give each teen a piece of paper and divide it into squares, one square for each **family member** including themselves. *(See Preteen Activity #13B.)*

Teen Activity #18B:
Make collages. *(See Preteen Activity #12B.)*

Teen Activity #19B:
Make a handout titled "Changes, changes, changes." *(See Preteen Activity #11B.)*

Teen Activity #20B:
Message in a bottle. *(See Preteen Activity #8B.)*

Teen Activity #21B:
Make memory boxes. These are to be used to place a special item that the loved one who died may have given the teens, or mementos of special times, or this could be a place to put notes or drawings to the deceased. *(See Preteen Activity #3B.)*

Teen Combined A and B Activities

Teen Activity (A&B) #1:
Have the teens bring in a **song**. *(See Preteen Activity A & B #2.)* The teens will **make a CD** representative of their loved ones.

Teen Activity (A&B) #2:
*Read: Poem "I Am." Using the same words as in the poem, have the teens complete their own "I Am" poem. *(See Preteen Activity A & B #3.)*

Teen Activity (A&B) #3:
Discuss wearing **masks** during grief. *(See Preteen Activity A & B #4.)* Use the papiermaché **masks** activity.

Teen Activity (A&B) #4:
Let the teens talk about the funeral. *(See Preteen Activity A & B#1.)* We have prepared cards (see addendum) asking **questions about the funeral**. Place these cards in a basket and encourage the teens to take a card and answer the question on the card.

Teen Activity (A&B) #5:

Use a **clothesline rope** and tie a knot for each teen in the group (If there are 10 teens, tie 10 knots. Tie them tight but not impossible to untie). Have each teen untie a knot as they talk about something that has made them **angry** since the death. The teen needs to keep talking for as long as it takes to untie the knot.

Optional: Using a **marker board**, have the teens make up a group list of people, situations, etc. that have made them **angry** since the death. Some examples from the teens are: the doctors (who may have seemed insensitive or may not have worked hard enough to save their loved one), ambulance drivers (who didn't get there fast enough), the drunk driver, God, the loved one for not being more careful, the loved one for smoking, other friends who still have their parent, sibling, etc., anger at classmates who say the wrong things or say nothing at all, anger at people who don't understand the depth of the loss, anger at ourselves, anger that others' lives go on but our lives feel stuck, etc.

Next, talk about things we can do when we feel **angry**. For example: jogging, swimming, hitting bed with pillow, basketball, listening to music, etc.

*Optional: Have the teens write a **letter** to the person(s) they are **angry** with and write what he/she would like to say to that person. The teens can choose to give that letter to the person or rip it up following this exercise.

– Thanksgiving –

CHILDREN'S ACTIVITY A   ***Read: <u>The Empty Place</u>** by R. Temes. In this story a child has died, and it is the first Thanksgiving since the death. (For young groups, read the book before you present it to the children and tell the story as you look at the pictures instead of reading the book.) Discussion topics: *What are some of the empty places for this boy? *What are some of the feelings that this boy has? *What are some of the feelings that you have had? *How do you think he feels about Thanksgiving this year? *How was the boy feeling at the end of the book?

CHILDREN' S ACTIVITY B   Make **turkeys**. Have children take colored construction paper and trace their hand. Make the thumb into a turkey's head (add eyes, a beak, and the wattle (the skin that hangs under the chin). For the fingers, the children are to write something that they are thankful for this year. (Facilitators — you may need to help the young ones who can't write well.)

OPTIONAL CHILDREN'S ACTIVITY B   Make **Indian Headdresses**. Give each child as many feathers as they like (most will need four or five). The idea is to make a feather for every person in the child's life that they are thankful for, including the person who has died. Let the children decorate the feathers and wear them as they leave group. Facilitators — please write "people we are thankful for" on the brown headband part of the headdress and help the children with writing if needed. Supplies: brown pieces (two per child) for headband, a variety of colored feathers, scissors, magic markers, and staplers.

PRETEEN ACTIVITY B   Take a dead tree (approximately 6-8') that has a lot of branches and using plaster of Paris secure it in a large pot. Have each preteen cut out a leaf from colored paper for each person in their life who has died (parent, grandparent, friend, etc.). After they have cut out a leaf, the preteen will draw veins on the leaf. Next the preteen will write on these veins his loved one's name and things that he/she thinks of when he thinks about the person who has died. Have the preteen share what he has written on the leaf and then tape the leaves on the tree.

TEEN ACTIVITY B   Use special fall-themed or leaf-patterned paper and make a handout with the following writing topics: Tell of a special Thanksgiving memory ..., Today I am thankful for ..., We are bits and pieces of our family members. I am like you when ..., I will always remember ..., and I want you to know ... .

– Christmas/Chanukah –

 CHILDREN'S ACTIVITY A **Read: <u>Holidays and Special Days</u> by J. Flynn. This is a coloring book that addresses for young children things they can do to remember their loved one during holidays and special days. You can purchase these for your children. Encourage your parents to color with their children and discuss these difficult days as they color the book together.

 **CHILDREN'S ACTIVITY B** Make **"Reindeer Pouches."** Supplies needed are red construction paper, brown construction paper, red yarn, big-eyed plastic needles, red pom-pom, two eyes, glue, notebook paper, and scissors. The children are to trace their hands on the red construction paper (both right and left) and cut them out. These are the reindeer's antlers. The children then trace one of their feet on two pieces of brown paper. These will be used for the reindeer's head. Next have the children sew together the two parts of the reindeer head with the red yarn. Then have the children glue on a "nose" (red pom-pom), the antlers, and two eyes. Note: the back piece of the brown face is cut smaller to allow a message to be put in the face. Next, with a facilitator's help depending on the age and ability of the child, have the child write a message or messages to the loved one who died to put in the reindeer.

 **OPTIONAL CHILDREN'S ACTIVITY B** Make **ginger bread men**. Supplies needed are brown construction paper, red paper for hearts, white yarn, big-eyed plastic needles, white rick-rack, eyes, buttons, glue, notebook paper, and scissors. Make a gingerbread man pattern and trace the gingerbread man on the brown construction paper. The children must first cut them out. Next have the child cut out a heart with the red paper. Then, have the facilitator punch holes on the heart so that the child can "sew" the heart on the gingerbread man (leaving the top of the heart not sewn) using yarn and the big-eyed plastic needles. Then use the eyes and buttons to make the gingerbread man's face. The white rick-rack can be glued by the hands and feet. Next, with facilitator's help depending on the age and ability of the child, have the child write a message to the loved one who died to place in the heart.

 **OPTIONAL CHILDREN'S ACTIVITY B** Have **cookies** for the children to decorate. Use frosting and sprinkles. As they decorate the cookie, encourage the children to talk about their loved one's favorite food (if they know what it is and if there are any food, restaurant, etc. memories). Supplies: knives, frosting, sprinkles, one cookie per person, and wax paper to work on.

OPTIONAL CHILDREN'S ACTIVITY B   Make **holiday ornaments**. You can purchase clear plastic 3" ornaments that come in two pieces so that a photo can be inserted into the ornament. Instruct the child to bring in a photo. Each child will get a plastic ornament, a white 3" circle, a silver 3" circle, and a piece of ribbon. You can purchase a cutter available at scrapbook supply stores that makes a perfect 3" circle. This is important because, to fit in the ornament, it must be a perfect cut. Purchase special markers for plastic. Place the opened ornament on the table and the children can draw a picture, write a message, etc. on the outside of one-half of the ornament. Next, using a glue stick, glue the photo to one side of the white circle and the silver circle to the other side of the white circle. Take the side of the ornament that has been decorated and lightly press the photo circle into it. If it is not pressed into the ornament, it will "flop" forward. Press the two halves of the ornament together and tie a ribbon in the hole on top.

PRETEEN ACTIVITY A   Discuss the upcoming **Christmas/Chanukah holiday.** Does anyone have any special traditions, special memories, or special stories? Does the family have plans to make the holiday different this year? For those who are celebrating the second holiday, does it feel different than last year? Talk about ways to get through the day. Do those who have already had other difficult days (birthdays, Father's Day, Mother's Day) have any suggestions that they can offer the other group members? For example, make a plan, do something totally different from tradition, invite someone over, or visit the cemetery?

PRETEEN ACTIVITY B   Make **holiday ornaments** (*See Children's Holiday Activity above*).

OPTIONAL PRETEEN ACTIVITY B   Make **luminaries**. Each preteen will get a can (large canned peaches or stewed tomatoes size). Have the preteens think of an item, design, etc. that reminds them of their loved one. They can use a washable marker to "dot" the design on the can. Then, using a hammer and nail and a piece of wood, have the preteen punch holes in the can following the design. (The wood needs to be slightly smaller than the size of the can so that it fits snugly in the can. Without the piece of wood it is difficult to drive nails into the can.) Some design ideas might include a religious symbol (cross or star), the loved one's initials, or an outline of an item; for example, a basketball, baseball, football, fish, bunny, etc. Once the can is completed, give each preteen a tea light (candle) and some fun tack adhesive (each preteen will need some fun tack only the size of a pea). Use the fun tack to stick the candle to the bottom of the can. Tell the preteens that these luminaries will be used after group for a special ceremony. After group, line the front walkway of your facility with the lighted luminaries and have a candlelight ceremony. The preteen and his/her family will stand by the luminary. Supplies: hammers, nails, can, wood, washable marker, tea light, and fun tack adhesive.

OPTIONAL PRETEEN ACTIVITY B Play the **holiday game** using questions written on paper cut out to look like holly leaves and candy canes. Have the preteen pick a holly leaf or candy cane game piece and answer the question. See addendum for questions.

OPTIONAL PRETEEN ACTIVITY B Make a **holiday ornament.** Dye Popsicle sticks yellow by following the directions on the dye box. The preteens can use these sticks to make a star. Have a sample of a "Christian" star and a "Jewish" star available. Use hot glue guns to glue the sticks together. Then the preteens are to write special things about the person who died on the front and the back of the stars. The preteens can also use glitter to decorate. Supplies needed: Popsicle sticks, glue guns, markers, glue, glitter, yarn or ribbon.

TEEN ACTIVITY A Discuss the upcoming **Christmas/Chanukah holiday.** Have the teens make a group list of things that their parent(s) can do to make the holiday easier for them this year. This activity helps open the door for discussion about things that are important for the teens during the holiday season. Some topics the teens have listed were make something in memory of the loved one, visiting the cemetery, continuing past holiday traditions of visiting the deceased parent's family, or possibly starting a new family tradition. Once the teens have completed this list, take this list and either make a copy to pass out to the adults or discuss the list in your adult group.

TEEN ACTIVITY B Make **holiday ornaments.** *(See Children's Holiday Activity on previous page.)*

OPTIONAL TEEN ACTIVITY B Make **luminaries.** *(See Preteen Holiday Activity on previous page.)*

OPTIONAL TEEN ACTIVITY B Play the **holiday game** *(See Preteen Holiday Activity on previous page.)*

– Valentine's Day –

CHILDREN'S ACTIVITY A   **Read: <u>Rachel and the Upside Down Heart</u>** by E. Douglas. In this book Rachel's father dies and her life changes in many ways. She and her mom move from their house in Kentucky to an apartment in New York. At first, Rachel feels so sad because her heart is upside down. After a while she meets new neighbors and friends. Discuss: Why did she make the heart upside down?

CHILDREN'S ACTIVITY B   Instruct the children to bring in a small photo of the loved one who died, a possession that belonged to the loved one, or something that reminds the child of the loved one. Make **valentines**. Take a Polaroid picture of the child with the item or photo and place in a photo holder that the children can decorate with foam colored hearts and magic markers.

PRETEEN ACTIVITY A   The preteens will bring in a small photo of the loved one who died or a possession that belonged to the loved one or reminds the preteen of the loved one. Make **valentines**. Take a Polaroid picture of the preteen with the item or photo and place in a photo holder that the preteens can decorate with foam colored hearts and magic markers. A suggestion for the preteens to decorate the photo holder is to have them spell their loved one's name vertically on the photo holder and then for each letter of the loved one's name, come up with an adjective that describes the loved one. For example if the loved one's name was Bill: For B the preteen might write "basketball", for I the preteen might write "intelligent," for L the preteen might write "loved" and for L the preteen might write "lawyer."

TEEN ACTIVITY A   Pass out red paper with hearts on it and encourage the teens to write a **valentine letter** to the person who died telling them what they continue to cherish and appreciate about that person.

Bibliography

Books

Blackburn, L.B. (1991). I know I made it happen. Omaha, NE: Centering Corporation.

Brown, L.K. & Brown, M. (1996). When dinosaurs die: A guide to understanding death. Boston: Little, Brown, & Co.

Brown, M. W., & Charlip, R. (1986). The dead bird. New York, NY: Harper Collins.

Cain, B.S. (1990). Double-dip feelings. New York, NY: Magination Press.

Carrick, C. (1988). The accident. New York, NY: Clarion Books.

Curtis, J.L. (1998). Today I feel silly. New York, NY: Harper Collins Publishers.

Czech, J. (2000). The garden angel. Omaha, NE: Centering Corporation.

Doleski, T. (1983). The hurt. Mahwah, NJ: Paulist Press.

Douglas, E. (1990). Rachel and the upside-down heart. Los Angeles: Price Stern Sloan.

Downey, R. (2001). Love is a family. New York, NY: Harper Collins Publishers, Inc.

Dr. Seuss (1998). My many colored days. New York, NY: Alfred A. Knopf.

Evans, L. (1999). Sometimes I feel like a storm cloud. Greenvale, NY: Mondo Publishing.

Flynn, J. (1994). Holidays and special days. Accord Aftercare Services.

Flynn, J. (1994). It's not your fault. Accord Aftercare Services.

Fox, M. (1998). Tough Boris. Orlando, FL: Harcourt Brace & Co.

Gackenbach, D. (1991). Alice's special room. Boston: Houghton Mifflin Co.

Greenlee, S. (1992). When someone dies. Atlanta: Peachtree Publishers, Ltd.

Grollman, E.A. (1993). Straight talk about death for teenagers. How to cope with losing someone you love. Boston, MA: Beacon Press Books.

Heegaard, M. (1991). When something terrible happens. Minneapolis, MN: Woodland Press.

Hemery, K. M. (1998). The brightest star. Omaha, NE: Centering Corporation.

Holmes, M. M. (1999). Molly's mom died. Omaha, NE: Centering Corporation.

Holmes, M. M. (2000). A terrible thing happened. Washington, DC: Magination Press.

Johnson, J. (1982). Where's Jess? Omaha, NE: Centering Corporation.

Lanton, S. (1991). Daddy's chair. Rockville, MD: Kar-Ben Copies.

Le Tord, B. (1987). My Grandma Leonie. New York, NY: Bradbury Press.

London, J. (1994). Liplap's wish. San Francisco: Chronicle Books.

Madenski, M. (1991). Some of the pieces. Boston: Little, Brown.

Marshall, B. (1998). Animal crackers. Omaha, NE: Centering Corporation.

MacGregor,C. (1999). Why do people die? Secaucus, NJ: Carol Publishing Group.

Mayer, M. (1983). I was so mad. Racine, WI: Western Publishing Co.

McLaughlin, K. (2001). The memory box. Omaha, NE: Centering Corporation.

Mellonie, B., & Ingpen, R. (1983). Lifetimes: The beautiful way to explain death to children. Toronto, Canada: Bantam Books.

Nobisso, J. (1990). Grandma's scrapbook. San Marcus, CA: Green Tiger Press.

Old, W. C. (1995). Stacy had a little sister. Morton Grove, Ill: Albert Whitman & Company.

Polland, B. K. (1975). Feelings: Inside you and outside too. San Francisco: Celestial Arts.

Powell, S. (1990). Geranium morning. Minneapolis, MN: Carolhoda Books.

Prestine, J. S. (1993). Someone special died. Parsippany, NJ: Fearon Teacher Aids.

Rugg, S. (1995). Memories live forever. Marietta, GA: Rising Sun Center for Loss and Renewal.

Sanford, D. (1986). It must hurt a lot. Portland, OR: Multnomah Press.

Scrivani, M. (1994). I heard your mommy died. Omaha, NE: Centering Corporation.

Scrivani, M. (1996). I heard your daddy died. Omaha, NE: Centering Corporation.

Simon, N. (1986). The saddest time. Morton Grove, IL: Albert Whitman.

Spelman, C. (1996). After Charlotte's mom died. Morton Grove, IL: Albert Whitman & Company.

Temes, R. (1992). The empty place: A child's guide through grief. Far Hills, NJ: Small Horizons.

Tiffault, B. W. (1983). A quilt for Elizabeth. Omaha, NE: Centering Corporation.

Vigna, J. (1991). Saying good-bye to Daddy. Morton Grove, IL: Albert Whitman.

Viorst, J. (1988). The tenth good thing about Barney. New York, NY: Macmillan.

Vogel, R. H. (1994), The snowman. Omaha, NE: Centering Corporation.

Wild, M. (1993). Toby. New York: Houghton Mifflin Co.

Wilhem, H. (1985). I'll always love you. New York, NY: Crown.

Wolfelt, A.D. (1996). How I feel: A coloring book for grieving children. Batesville, IN: Batesville Management Services.

Yeomans, E. (2000). Lost and found: Remembering a sister. Omaha, NE: Centering Corporation.

Yolen, J. (1994). Granddad Bill's song. New York, NY: Philomel Books.

Zolotow, C. (1974). My Grandson Lew. New York, NY: Harper Trophy.

Video

Based on the book by Judith Viorst, The tenth good thing about Barney. Chatsworth, CA: AIMS Media.

Tape

Cassette audio tape. Friends of the family. (1988). Bedford, TX: Celebration Shop, Inc. For ordering information call (817) 268-0020.

Cassette audio tape. Mr. Al Sings Friends and Feelings. Melody House. For ordering information write Melody House, 819 NW 92nd Street, Oklahoma City, Ok 73114.

**For information on obtaining some of the above mentioned books,
or books on similar subjects, contact:**
• The Centering Corporation, www.centering.org or call (402) 553-1200.
• Accord Inc., www.accordinc.org or call (800) 346-3087.

Addendum

Questions for soccer ball game
- How have your activities — Scouts, sports, etc. — been affected by the death?
- How are you different since the death?
- Do you think about your own death?
- Tell of a time when you have felt different since the death.
- Tell us something that you are proud of.
- If your parent died, what do you think about your surviving parent dating?
- If your friend's loved one died, what would you say to him/her?
- What would you change about the funeral?
- What did your loved one wear in the casket?
- If you could have left a special item in the casket, what would it have been?
- Do you worry about someone else dying?
- What have been some unhelpful things people have said/done?
- Tell of a thing that has made you angry since the death.
- How do you feel when your parent cries?
- Tell of a funny memory about your loved one.
- What do you miss the most about your loved one?

Questions for holiday game
- What is your favorite part of the holiday season?
- What do you like the least about the holiday season?
- What do you fear the most about the holidays?
- What will be the most difficult thing you will have to do during the holidays without your loved one?
- What can you do to feel close to your loved one this holiday season?
- Discuss a holiday tradition that you want your family to continue.
- Share a special holiday memory.
- How are you feeling tonight as you look toward the holidays?
- How can your friends help you this holiday season?
- Share a silly holiday memory.
- If you could change something about a past holiday, what would it be?
- What could be a way that you and/or your family can remember your loved one during the holiday season?
- Are there any traditions that you want to change this holiday season?

Grief game questions
- What changes have you noticed in your family members since the death?
- What can you do to make sure you remember the person who died?
- Before the death, my most loved possession was ... Today, my most loved possession is ...
- I miss doing_____ with the person who died.
- Describe your loved one to the group.
- How do you feel when someone says, "I know just what you're going through"?
- Do family members grieve the same way you do? If not, how do they grieve differently?
- Tell something about yourself that you are proud of.
- What family tradition has changed since the death?
- If you could have put an item in the casket, what would you have chosen?
- How did you feel about coming to this group your first night?
- In what ways have your relationships with friends changed since the death?
- If you could change a part of the funeral, what would it be?
- What do you miss the most about your loved one?
- What have you discovered about grief since your loved one died?
- If you could see your loved one one more time, what would you like to say to him/her?
- In what way are you like your mother?
- In what way are you like your father?
- Share something that your loved one taught you.
- What has been the most difficult thing you have had to deal with since your loved one died?
- Complete this sentence: "I wish I had ... "

- Has your attitude about what is important in life changed since the death?
- What advice have you received that was helpful for you in coping with your grief?
- Where do you go to feel close to your loved one?
- What was the most difficult thing for you to handle at the funeral?
- Before the death, my biggest fear was … Today, my biggest fear is …
- Share a fear or worry you have had since the death.
- Who/what has helped you the most since the death?
- What advice would you give a new member to this group?
- Share a favorite family memory.
- Complete this sentence: "One of the ways I make it difficult for people to talk to me about the death or my feelings is …"
- What has changed in your household since your loved one died?

Funeral questions
- What is one thing you wish you could have changed about the funeral?
- What were the songs used at the funeral?
- Have you ever heard of anyone leaving a gift in the casket? What do you think of this idea? If you could have left a gift, what would it have been?
- What did your loved one wear in the casket?
- How did your family decide which cemetery to use?
- Were you involved in any of the plans for the funeral? If so, what part?
- Tell about your first visit to the cemetery.
- What happened following the funeral?
- What did your minister/priest/rabbi do?
- Tell about the people who attended the funeral/service. (Special friends, family, a lot of people, of just a small group?)
- Tell about the visitation or viewing.
- I did _____ at the service.
- Describe what the funeral home looked like.
- What was the hardest part of the day of the funeral?
- What was the hardest part of the funeral?

Questions for Jenga game
- My first experience with death was when_____.
- Share how the death is discussed in your home.
- To the best of your memory, at what age were you first aware of death?
- What do you think happens after death?
- Do you think about your own death?
- If you could pick an age to die, what would it be? Why?
- If you could choose how you would die, how would it be?
- When do you think you will die?
- What type of funeral do you want for yourself?
- Would you be willing to donate an organ after you die?
- What do you think about open casket funerals?
- If your parent died, what do you think about your surviving parent dating?
- What is better now than it was just after the death?
- If your friend's loved one died, what would you say to him/her?
- How important is the ritual of a funeral/memorial service?
- If you were told you have a terminal disease, would you change anything about your life?
- Has there been a time in your life when you wanted to die?
- If you knew a friend was suicidal, what would you do?
- What would you change about the funeral?
- What did your loved one wear in the casket?
- Was there special music at the funeral?
- Were you involved in the planning of the funeral? If so, what part?
- Have you ever heard of anyone leaving a "gift" in the casket? What do you think of this idea?
- What was the hardest part of the day of the funeral?
- What was the most positive thing you remember about the funeral?
- At the time of the death, who was the most helpful?

Complete this statement: I feel alone when _____.	Complete this statement: I feel guilty when I _____.	When your loved one died, what were some of the reactions of the adults around you? How did their reactions make you feel?
Did your parent(s) buffer you (protect you) in any way when your loved one died or was dying?	When your loved one died (or was dying) were any emotions encouraged or discouraged? By whom? How?	Tell of something that has made you angry since the death. What can you do with your anger so that you don't carry it with you for the rest of your life?
Have your beliefs or understanding about death changed since your loved one died?	Tell us how your family has changed since the death.	Tell of a way you have changed since the death.
Which adults positively or negatively impressed you with their reaction to the death?	Has anyone said anything that helped or comforted you since the death? Tell us what they said or did.	Is there a smell that reminds you of your loved one?

Has anyone said or done anything that irritated or angered you? Tell us what they said or did.	Is there a special place that reminds you of your loved one?	Tell us a way you are like (similar to) your loved one.
What do you want others to understand about you and how you feel about the death?	How has your everyday routine changed since the death?	Did your loved one have a favorite food or restaurant? What was it? How do you feel when you eat that special food now?
What is the one thing you think the person who died would like to know?	Complete this statement: I could feel better if only I could _____.	When you think about what happened, what is one thing you are thankful for?
If you could change something about the death or when he/she was dying (other than having the person alive and well), what would it be?	Complete this statement: When I let my feelings out, I _____.	What is one thing you wish you had not done?

What do you think is the most important thing(s) that you learned from the one who died?	What is something that you can do now to show your love for the one who died?	If you could tell the person who died just one thing, what would it be?
Complete this statement: I think what I need most now is _____.	Which people were the most difficult to tell that your loved one died? Why?	What reactions have you gotten from people when you tell them about your loved one who died?
If you had a friend who had a loved one die, what advice would you give them that you wish someone had said to you?	How does being in your house feel now that your loved one died? Is it still home?	Is there a place you now avoid since your loved one died?
Who told you your loved one died or was dying?	Complete this statement: When I hear my loved's name mentioned, I _____.	Complete this statement: The last thing I remember I did with my loved one was _____.

Complete this statement: Since my loved one's death, my life _____.	Complete this statement: I wish I had _____.	Complete this statement: I wish you (the person who died) had _____.
Complete this statement: My greatest surprise since my loved one died is _____.	Complete this statement: I find it hard to forgive _____.	Complete this statement: What scares me most is _____.
If you have had a dream about your loved one who died, tell us about it. If you have not, what would you like the dream to be?	How do you think your life would be different now if your loved one was still alive?	Complete this statement: I miss _____.
Complete this statement: When I think of my loved one who died, I don't miss _____.	Has anyone lied to you since the death or about details of the death? How did that feel?	Sometimes your pain may seem different from what others say about theirs. Have you ever experienced this? How did you feel?

Do you think people treat you differently now that you have had a loss?	Sometimes after a loved one has died, people wear an article of clothing or a piece of jewelry or carry a special memento that belonged to the person who died. Some people call this a "comfort" item. Do you have such an item? If you don't what would it be?	The news of a death can leave you thinking that it really didn't happen. This is called denial. Has this happened to you?
Have you ever felt ashamed of your feelings about your loss? Tell us about that.	Is there a song that comes to mind when you think of your loved one? Do you use music to help you cope with your grief?	Have you ever felt responsible or blamed yourself for your loved one's death?
Complete this statement: "The biggest loss or change (other than the death of my loved one) to my life has been ..."	In what ways have your hopes and plans for the future changed as a result of the death?	Have your relationships with your friends changed as a result of the death? Who has been a good friend and what do they do to be a good friend to you?
Complete this statement: "It isn't easy for me to admit ..."	Have your attitudes toward what is most important in life changed as a result of the death? If so, in what ways?	Complete this statement: I wish my teachers could understand ...

When you need to talk to someone, who do you go to? If you haven't reached out to someone, is there someone who you might want to try to reach out to?	Complete this statement: "One of the ways I make it difficult for people to talk to me about the death or my feelings is ..."	How do you feel when someone says, "I know just what you're going through"?
Complete this statement: My biggest fear or concern since the death is _____.	Complete this statement: I wish my parent(s) could understand that _____.	Tell of a time when you have felt different or uncomfortable at school.
Is there something that you do by yourself now that you used to do with your loved one?		

– Index –

How to Order Directly from the Publisher

Book Price: $24.95

Please send _____copies of Healing Activities for Children in Grief to:

Name _____

Agency _____

Address _____

City _____ State _____ Zip _____

Please complete order details:

_____ Copies @ $24.95 per copy	=	$_____
TX Residents Add 8 ½% Sales Tax	=	$_____
Shipping and Handling ($5.00 per book)	=	$_____
Enclosed Is a Check For Total		$_____

Make Check Payable to/Mail to:
Gay McWhorter
1713 Bellechase Drive
Roanoke, Texas 76262
(817) 379-5544
FAX (817) 431-7085
email address: griefactivities@aol.com